ULTIMATE CLEVELAND INDIANS TIME MACHINE BOOK

MARTIN GITLIN

LYONS PRESS

Guilford, Connecticut

An imprint of The Rowman & Littlefield Publishing Group, Inc.
4501 Forbes Blvd., Ste. 200
Lanham, MD 20706
www.rowman.com

Distributed by NATIONAL BOOK NETWORK

Copyright © 2019 Martin Gitlin

All rights reserved. No part of this book may be reproduced in any form or by any electronic or mechanical means, including information storage and retrieval systems, without written permission from the publisher, except by a reviewer who may quote passages in a review.

British Library Cataloguing in Publication Information available

Library of Congress Cataloging-in-Publication Data available

Names: Gitlin, Marty, author.
Title: Ultimate Cleveland Indians time machine book / Martin Gitlin.
Description: Guilford, Connecticut : Lyons Press, [2019] | Includes
  bibliographical references.
Identifiers: LCCN 2018052777 (print) | LCCN 2018059227 (ebook) | ISBN
  9781493040230 (ebook) | ISBN 9781493040223 | ISBN 9781493040223(paperback) |
  ISBN 9781493040230(e-book)
Subjects: LCSH: Cleveland Indians (Baseball team)—History.
Classification: LCC GV875.C7 (ebook) | LCC GV875.C7 G57 2019 (print) | DDC
  796.357/6477132—dc23
LC record available at https://lccn.loc.gov/2018052777

♾™ The paper used in this publication meets the minimum requirements of American National Standard for Information Sciences—Permanence of Paper for Printed Library Materials, ANSI/NISO Z39.48-1992.

Printed in the United States of America

Contents

Contents

Introduction

OCTOBER 28, 1995. WORLD SERIES. GAME 6. ATLANTA FULTON COUNTY Stadium. Press box.

Witnessing the demise of that year's edition of the Indians under the weight of stellar Braves pitching as a sports journalist, I understood three things:

1. I had to work fast procuring quotes in the locker room to make deadline.

2. I had to sustain objectivity in my writing and reporting.

3. I felt like crying.

My task as a sportswriter was slowed by the emotions of Cleveland players shedding tears through their words while being interviewed. I found myself hoping against hope they would stop weeping long enough to give me a few cogent sentences, but I understood their emotional pain. I was feeling heartbreak as well. I could always preserve impartiality in my game stories but could no more maintain it in my heart than I could stop breathing.

I was and will always be an Indians fan. My passion for the team, born in the early 1960s, strengthened even through the misery of three barren decades and disappointment of failed opportunities, never prevented me from remaining unbiased as a journalist. In fact, I have argued, the depth of my personal fandom has made me more, not less, critical of the franchise as it continued to search for that elusive World Series championship.

And, as always, there are the memories. I recall vividly most of the entries in this Indians time machine. I was just three when Rocky Colavito was stupidly and recklessly dispatched to the Tigers, but I remember my joy when he returned. Little could my eight-year-old mind compute that the trade that brought him back could prove more devastating than the one that shipped him out. I remember Sudden Sam McDowell losing games he should have won by throwing curves to .180 hitters he could have blown away with fastballs. I never dreamed that his career was slowly being ruined by alcohol. Nobody did. There was the tragedy of Tony Horton and the thrill of Frank Robinson's Opening Day blast. My childhood was rich with memories both horrible and wonderful.

Such events during the darkest days served only to fortify my love for the Indians. Those that grace the pages of this book, some of which were experienced by generations before mine, helped form the storied history of the Cleveland Indians. It has indeed been a roller coaster ride, the gloom of the 1960s through the early 1990s lasting far longer than the sustained joys of the 1940s, 1950s, 1990s, and the modern-day Terry Francona years.

It has been said that only through experiencing feelings of misery can one fully appreciate happiness. The same can be claimed about Indians fans. Certainly, those too young to have known the annual heartaches of the Curse of the Rocky Colavito decades still felt delight when the team exploded into greatness in the 1990s at shiny new Jacobs Field. But that glee could never have reached the same level in younger fans as it did in those who maintained their love and passion for the Indians through their worst era.

This book, however, is for all Cleveland fans—all baseball fans, really. Even those who root for other teams can identify with the trials and tribulations of the Indians over more than a century. Readers will recall with relish the moments, the players, the teams they embraced in both their childhood and adult years.

Enjoy.

Chapter One

The Sinking, Stinking Spiders

The 1962 New York Mets have been forever deemed the poster child for incompetence since compiling a 40–120 record in that inaugural season. But accompanying the word "ineptitude" in the dictionary should be a team photo of the 1899 Cleveland Spiders. They made the Mets look like the 1927 Yankees.

The tangled web spun by Spiders owner and local streetcar mogul Frank Robison was created quickly and motivated by greed. The National League team had proven itself artistically successful. Cleveland posted winning records in each of the previous seven seasons and placed second in 1892, 1895, and 1896. But the Spiders ranked near the bottom in attendance every year, falling to dead last in 1897 and 1898.[1]

Robison believed the lowly St. Louis franchise would attract stronger fan support with a better team. So under the then-current National League rules, which allowed owners to own stock in multiple teams, he transferred premier Spiders talent to the Browns. Included was immortal right-hander Cy Young, fresh off a 25-win season and after whom the annual award for pitching excellence is named. Among those also hijacked were .400-hitting outfielder Jesse Burkett and fellow future Hall of Famer Bobby Wallace, who led the Spiders with 99 runs batted in 1898.[2]

Nary a bum was targeted in the transfer. Included among those shipped to Missouri was a second baseman with the lovely name of Cupid Childs, who had averaged 118 runs scored in eight seasons for the Spiders. Jack Powell had won 23 games the year before. Shortstop Ed McKean

Owner Frank Robison crushed the Spiders in 1899 by shipping their best players to St. Louis.

smashed a team-high nine home runs, a prodigious total in the dead ball era that placed him fourth in the National League. Even player-manager Patsy Tebeau proved vulnerable. He too was ordered by Robison to literally follow the words of Horace Greeley: "Go west, young man."

Robison could hardly be blamed for taking radical action, though his purchase of the Browns while remaining in control of the Spiders certainly strayed into the territory of vengeful business. He had grown hateful of Cleveland fans, whose lack of support resulted in him barely making payroll in 1898. He at first denied interest in buying the Browns, claiming in what today would be politically incorrect terms that such a rumor "had originated in some Chinese laundry." But he soon jumped on the opportunity to purchase the St. Louis franchise at a meager cost when it filed for bankruptcy.

Tebeau sought to soothe the albeit small Cleveland fan base by promising that Robison would not raid the roster and predicting a "banner season" for the Spiders. But two weeks later and a mere 17 days before the launch of the regular season, Robison indeed transferred his best to a St. Louis team he had renamed the Perfectos. What had become known as "syndicate baseball" was about to transform a strong group into more than a laughingstock. The lone player that took the opposite route from St. Louis to Cleveland was second baseman Lave Cross, who was named player-manager. And *he* was returned to the Perfectos early in the season. Simply and irrefutably stated, the 1899 Spiders were the worst team in the history of the sport.

That the team opened the regular season in St. Louis served to rub salt in the wound. That wound became more painful after a 10–1 shellacking by the Perfectos that exposed weaknesses in all areas of the game that the Spiders would prove unable to repair the rest of the year. They allowed an absurd average of 10 runs in their first eight games and soon embarked on an 11-game losing streak that dropped their record to 3–20. While Robison whistled in the dark by praising the spirit of the club and predicting emergence from the funk, his team would remain so deeply entrenched in the cellar that fans launched a boycott. A paltry average of 145 masochistic fans trickled into League Park to watch the seemingly daily slaughter.[3]

National League rivals soon refused to make the trip because their take of ticket revenue proved smaller than their travel expenses. Robison, whose boast that his Spiders would fly once they rounded into condition merited the same level of credence of a claim that pigs could fly, soon raised the white flag. He sent Cross, the team's only .300 hitter, packing to St. Louis after Cleveland dropped to 8–30. Robison blamed umpires for the galling record while taking a shot at what he intimated was an unappreciative fan base. "I cannot keep running a club with a salary list of $30,000 for an attendance of 100 a day," he grumbled. He replaced Cross with Joe Quinn, the first Australian-born player in the majors.[4]

Playing in a virtual vacuum proved impossible. The Spiders crawled away from home from late May forward, transforming themselves into permanent road warriors. They played just eight home games the rest of the year while serving as a punching bag for National League competition. They battled epic bouts of futility. They lost 13 in a row in early June. They dropped 14 straight in July. They ran off 11 consecutive defeats a month later. Cleveland sportswriters derided the traveling circus as "misfits" and "exiles." *Sporting Life* correspondent Elmer Bates joked that Clevelanders should take a glass-half-full approach to their fandom. After all, they no longer had to be concerned that a rival would pass the Spiders in the standings, nor were they ever bothered by others asking them the score of a game because everyone assumed they were losing.[5]

Opposing teams felt more pressure to win than the lost-cause Spiders. Among those who felt the wrath of management was Baltimore pitcher Jerry Nops, who apparently believed he could beat Cleveland in June with a hangover. The result was a defeat that motivated his eventually legendary manager John McGraw to fine and suspend him. The ashamed Orioles responded in the next game by stomping the Spiders, 21–6.[6]

"The players are doing the best they can and only ask that the spectators use no firearms," wryly offered *The Sporting News*[7] before the almost-permanent exodus. The Spiders did return to Cleveland in late August for games against the New York Giants and Boston Beaneaters after spending seven consecutive weeks on the road. The two teams refused to host the Spiders for series that were supposed to be played in Cleveland. The result, as one might expect, was six defeats in seven games and the beginning of an epic 24-game losing streak that remains a National League record.

That skein concluded in a monumental collapse. The day of infamy was September 16. The place was Boundary Field. The opponent was the Washington Senators. Only 400 fans showed up to witness what resulted in history. The Spiders had been outscored 194–55 in losing 23 straight. They had fallen behind permanently in the first inning of 10 of those defeats and such a scenario seemed possible again when Washington scored a run immediately. But the Spiders exploded for eight runs in the second inning on six hits and three Senator errors.

Cleveland, however, was not a team that could stand prosperity. Its offense shut down while Washington chipped away and forged ahead 11–8 with a five-run eighth. The Spiders never recovered, falling 15–10 to establish a mark that has remained intact for nearly 12 decades. Winning pitcher Jack Fifield certainly remembered it fondly—it was the only victory of his career. But then, the 1899 Spiders aided in many players achieving lifelong highlights.[8]

The Spiders won their next game, then lost their last 16. They had dropped 40 of 41, a stretch of ineptitude unmatched in baseball history. And they went out with a flourish. They summoned 19-year-old local amateur pitcher Eddie Kolb to hurl the season finale. His only relationship to the Spiders was as a cigar boy at the Cincinnati hotel in which they were staying. The result was certainly predictable. The Reds pounded Kolb en route to a 19–3 shellacking that finally, gratefully, put the Spiders out of their misery.[9]

History, however, keeps them alive. And statistics scream out the woeful tale. The Spiders finished an incredible 84 games out of first place and 35 games behind second-last Washington. They finished 11–101 on the road—that number of defeats away from home will remain a major league record forever, as teams now play only 81 road games.

Not one pitcher on the outrageously horrific staff won more than four games. "Ace" Jim Hughley finished with a 4–30 record and 5.41 earned run average. Not bad considering the team finished with a 6.37 ERA, nearly double the league average. The Spiders allowed a major league record 1,252 runs, an average of 8.2 per game, and more than 13 hits per nine innings. Starters Charlie Knepper, Frederick "Crazy" Schmidt, and Harry Colliflower (who compiled a disturbing 8.17 ERA) combined for a 7–50 record.

The hitting was better—but not by much. The Spiders scored 529 runs, an average of 3.4 per game. Their .253 team batting mark was 29 points below the league average. They managed just 12 home runs on the season, atypical even in the dead ball era. Wallace alone slugged that many that year with the Perfectos. The Spiders placed last in the National League in runs, hits, doubles, triples, home runs, walks, batting average, on-base percentage, and slugging percentage.[10]

Cleveland fans angered by the betrayal of Robison, who had stopped paying Spiders players in mid-August before finally compensating them off in November, did receive a small level of consolation that the Perfectos were far from perfect. They did not achieve the intended benefits of his player maneuverings. Though they beat the Spiders in 13 of 14 meetings (who didn't?) and finished second in the National League in attendance, they placed fifth in the standings and fell out of the pennant race by mid-June. They won just five more games than they lost against teams not called the Cleveland Spiders.[11]

The Spiders received no opportunity to rebound. They were among four teams dropped from the National League after the 1899 season. But Cleveland was not without baseball for long. The city became a charter member of the fledgling American League in 1901. And its experience with Robison motivated a change for the better. What became known as syndicate baseball was banned by the National League. The wholesale movement of players by owners of multiple teams could no longer sully the reputation of the Grand Old Game and create a competitive imbalance.

In the total scope of baseball immortality, the Spiders rank high among Cleveland teams. And perhaps that is a good thing. For nearly 120 years later, their haplessness translates not into anxiety and emotional pain, but rather a good laugh. That 1899 season was at least one to remember. After all, that was the year the Spiders earned the title of Worst Team in Baseball History.

CHAPTER TWO

The Loss of Joss

IT WAS 1911, 28 YEARS BEFORE LOU GEHRIG GAVE THE MOST STORIED and courageous speech in baseball history as a man consumed not by his destiny on death's door, but by his good fortune to have played with the New York Yankees. Indeed, more than a quarter century before "the luckiest man on the face of the earth" talked his way into the hearts of America, even those who cared little about sports, the Indians experienced their own tragedy that befell a beloved player.

That player was Addie Joss. The brilliant right-handed pitcher died at age 31 on April 14, 1911, the victim of tubercular meningitis. Joss was so revered by his teammates and foes that his death inspired the threat of a players' strike and the first all-star game in the history of the sport.[1]

The all-too-short life of Addie Joss began 31 years earlier, almost to the day of his passing. He was born on April 12, 1880, in Woodland, Wisconsin, the lone offspring of Jacob and Theresa Joss. His father was a Swiss immigrant whose relocation to that part of the United States was inspired by a desire to dabble in the cheese-making trade. Jacob had become adept enough in his profession to own his own factory in his new hometown. But though he conquered his professional pursuits, he could not conquer his battle with the bottle. Jacob died of alcoholism when his son was a mere 10 years old. That forced his mother to open a millinery shop and sewing school in nearby Juneau, Wisconsin, to make ends meet.[2]

So tall and skinny had her son developed that he gained unflattering, but appropriate nicknames such as the Human Slat and the Human

Adrian ("Addie") Joss

These frame-by-frame photos show the windup and delivery that made Addie Joss an all-time great.

WIKIMEDIA COMMONS, COURTESY OF LOUIE VAN OEYEN

Hairpin. And though his physique proved ideal for a pitcher, he launched his baseball career as a second baseman on the Juneau High School team. Upon graduation at the tender age of 16, he joined the teaching profession in the nearby town of Horicon but remained active on the diamond. He joined the baseball team in that town as a pitcher and established a unique motion that would emerge as his calling card throughout his career. Joss turned his body toward second base, kicked his leg skyward, yet remained upright following his delivery. That allowed him to establish ideal fielding position.[3]

Joss joined a financially struggling franchise in Oshkosh in 1899 that froze player salaries, including his at a mere $10 per week. After that team was disbanded, he hooked up with a secondary club in Manitowoc as a second baseman before earning a spot on the mound with its premier team and forging a record of 4–1. He was soon discovered by Charles J. Strobel, owner of the Toledo club of the Inter-State League, who offered Joss his first professional contract.[4]

So taken was the Toledo manager with the talent of Joss that he tabbed the just-turned-20-year-old as his Opening Day starter. He was not sorry he did. And neither was Joss—for more than one reason. He not only earned his first victory, but among the attendees was Lillian Shinavar, who would become his wife in 1902. Lillian began dating one of the finest pitching prospects in baseball. Joss recorded a mark of 19–16 in his first pro season, then totaled 25 victories and 216 strikeouts a year later. Though he remained thin, he had filled out to a more strapping 6-foot-3, 185 pounds. It came as no surprise when the Cleveland Bronchos of the American League invited him to spring training in 1902.[5]

His performance there was enough to convince manager Bill Armour to plug Joss into his rotation. Joss began with a bang, taking a no-hitter into the sixth inning against the St. Louis Browns and finishing with a one-hit, 3–0 victory. He finished that season with a league-leading five shutouts, 17–14 record, and strong 2.77 earned run average. He proved so adept at a mere 22 years old that he was invited to compete with fellow American League standouts in a winter tour.[6]

Joss took his momentum and ran with it, improving markedly his next two seasons in establishing himself as one of the premier pitchers in the game. He dropped his ERA more than a half point in 1903, leading the league in WHIP (walks and hits to innings pitched) and topping one and all in ERA in 1904 (during which he allowed no home runs) despite a distinct lack of hitting support. He had already emerged as one of the stingiest pitchers in baseball history. He managed his first 20-win season in 1905, then posted ERAs under 1.84 over each of the next four years.

But Joss proved more than one-dimensional. He landed an offseason job as a Sunday sports columnist with the *Toledo News Bee* after the 1906 season. He wrote about serious issues, as well as humorous anecdotes from his own experiences in baseball. He even covered the World Series. It was no wonder that he gained favor with fans, who backed him during his holdout for a salary increase before the 1907 season that resulted in a hefty (for that time) $4,000 contract. He peaked in 1908 with a 24–11 record and 1.16 ERA, which remains the eighth-best ever in the major leagues.[7]

Joss pored over engineering books following that season before designing an electronic scoreboard called the Joss Indicator that was eventually installed at League Park in Cleveland. It provided fans the opportunity to track balls and strikes and posted the lineups of both teams.

It was no solitary achievement or statistic, but rather a single performance that will forever be most remembered about Joss's career. The date was October 2, 1908. The Naps and White Sox, in the stretch run of a heated pennant chase with Detroit, battled on a cool Cleveland afternoon. Chicago sent future Hall of Famer Ed Walsh to the mound. He performed brilliantly in seeking his 40th victory that year, yielding just one unearned run and four hits while striking out 15. But his effort paled in comparison to that of Joss, who retired all 27 Sox he faced for the second perfect game in baseball history—a perfect game before the term "perfect game" had ever been uttered. The Naps might have tied the Tigers for the title, but a rainout game was never rescheduled, per the rules of the era, and they finished a half game behind.[8]

Joss maintained his status as ace of a bad Cleveland team in 1909, but hauntingly suffered from fatigue throughout that season. He pitched more than 80 fewer innings than he had in 1908 and his strikeouts dipped dramatically. He appeared to have regained his strength to begin the following year, tossing a no-hitter on April 20, again against the White Sox. He continued to pitch well but was eventually sidelined by a torn ligament in his right elbow. He hurled his last game in late July 1910. Little could anyone have imagined that it would be the final regular-season performance of his career.[9]

The arm problems never dissipated. He planned to return to the mound in May 1911 after resting it. But as the Naps returned north from spring training and stopped in Chattanooga for an exhibition game against the minor league Lookouts, he fainted while talking to old friend Rudy Hulswitt, a shortstop on the opposing team. Joss was dispatched to his hometown of Toledo, where, after being diagnosed with tubercular meningitis, his condition continued to deteriorate. Eleven days after his collapse and two days after his 31st birthday, Addie Joss was dead.

His teammates were stunned. So were the pitchers, hitters, coaches, and managers he had spent the last nine years dominating. The entire Naps roster planned to attend his funeral on April 17. But American League president Ban Johnson refused to cancel their scheduled game in Detroit. The infuriated band of players ignored the edict, threatening to sign a petition and hopping on a train to Toledo in direct defiance of Johnson's orders. The *Detroit News* callously called their actions a "mutiny" while others deemed it a strike. But the huge majority of media members wrote editorials backing the players, blasting Johnson for his heartlessness and offering that devotion to a beloved fallen teammate usurped any obligation to play a comparatively meaningless early regular-season game. Johnson eventually relented, rescheduling it for later that year.[10]

The enormity of the event became evident when famed evangelist and former major league outfielder Billy Sunday delivered the eulogy. Sunday was effusive in his praise for Joss, using baseball analogies to describe his fight against the inevitable.

"Joss tried hard to strike out death, and it seemed for a time as though he would win," Sunday eulogized. "The bases were full. The score was a tie, with two outs. Thousands, yes millions, in a nation's grandstands and bleachers sat breathless watching the conflict. The great twirler stood erect in the box. Death walked to the plate."[11]

All-Stars came far and wide to honor the fallen Addie Joss in 1911.

WIKIMEDIA COMMONS, COURTESY OF LOUIE VAN OEYEN

Johnson had finally come around to the impact of Joss's passing. He green-lighted a plan by Naps president C. W. Summers to schedule a special game between Cleveland players and the premier American League talent on July 24, which would be known as Addie Joss Day. The proceeds from the event would be donated to his widow and two children. So enamored had his peers been with Joss that they all agreed to participate. Even nasty Ty Cobb, perhaps the most hated player in baseball history, agreed to attend.

It was the first collection of premier talent ever assembled—the inaugural All-Star Game would not be played for more than two decades. The battle at League Park drew a then-huge crowd of 15,270. Their purchase of tickets and scorecards, as well as contributions from National League representatives, resulted in $13,000 provided to the Joss family. Such superstars of the era as Cobb, Eddie Collins, Sam Crawford, Tris Speaker, Shoeless Joe Jackson, Walter Johnson, Nap Lajoie, and Naps starting pitcher Cy Young graced the field that day.[12]

Not only had Joss earned legend as arguably the greatest pitcher in Cleveland baseball history despite his tragedy-shortened career—he statistically bested even the immortal Bob Feller—but the game inspired by his death planted the seeds for other such classics. The concept of an all-star battle between the American and National Leagues was raised again just four years later by *Baseball Magazine* editor F. C. Lane, who called the potential contest "the real grand Opera of baseball." Though the idea did not take, it was just a matter of time before *Chicago Tribune* sports editor Arch Ward provided the impetus for the annual All-Star Game, which was launched in 1933.

Joss would not be forgotten. He was finally chosen by the Veterans Committee for the Hall of Fame in 1978. And nearly 40 years later, television network Sports Time Ohio produced an homage to the pitcher titled *Addie Joss: Revealed*. The highly acclaimed documentary highlighted his perfect game in 1908 and his untimely passing, as well as the love and admiration he had gained from his peers. Not only was it narrated by Indians play-by-play broadcaster Matt Underwood, but passages were read by such current Indians standouts as All-Star Corey Kluber, who in his own right had established himself as a rival of Joss as one of the finest hurlers ever to wear a Cleveland uniform.

Joss finished his career with a 160–97 record and 1.89 ERA that ranks second in Major League Baseball history to Walsh, ironically. More impressive is that Joss's career WHIP of 0.968 is the best. Given those numbers and the likelihood that Joss would have flirted with 300 wins had his career not been cut short, that it took more than six decades for him to be elected into the Hall seems shocking. But not as shocking as his sudden passing in 1911.

CHAPTER THREE

Tragedy and Triumph

SOMETHING DIFFERENT WAS HAPPENING IN 1920. WITH THE TEAM now known as the Indians in honor of Native American Louis Sockalexis, a former Tribe player and member of the Penobscot tribe of Maine, there were hints that this season would be special as it reached its halfway point.

The Indians were tied for first place on Independence Day. But that was far from shocking considering that for two consecutive years they were at least in the periphery of the pennant race. What piqued interest and whet appetites were individual performances on the field. It had nothing to do with Tris Speaker. He was on his way to batting .388, but his brilliance was a given. It was more about fellow outfielder Elmer Smith, who was blossoming en route to a 103-RBI season. And nondescript infielder Larry Gardner, who at age 34 was about to add 32 RBI to his largest career output. And pitcher Jim Bagby, who had never previously and would never again approach the victory total of 31 he would achieve that year.

Something was indeed happening in 1920 and Cleveland fans streamed to the ballpark in larger numbers than ever. Nearly one million fans converged on League Park as the team sought its first pennant. World War I was over, the Roaring Twenties was about to begin, and Indians fans were ready to celebrate. It had become apparent early that year that only the White Sox and Yankees stood in their way.

A critical battle with Babe Ruth's bunch on August 16 awaited at the Polo Grounds, which the Yankees shared with the National League

Southpaw Stan Coveleski won 24 games for the title-winning Tribe in 1920.

Giants until they moved into their own iconic stadium three years later. The Indians stood a half game ahead of Chicago and a game and a half in front of the Bronx Bombers heading into that afternoon battle. It was a drizzly, dark Monday, but it was about to get much gloomier, at least figuratively.

Ace Carl Mays toed the rubber that day for New York in search of his 100th career victory. The submarine-style right-hander had earned a nasty reputation as a headhunter. His motion, in which his knuckles nearly scraped the dirt before release, not only made him tough to hit, but downright scary for right-handed batters. Mays jammed foes as a weapon, but boasted pinpoint control, averaging just two walks per nine innings throughout his career. That he annually placed among the American League leaders in hit batsmen despite his accuracy indicated that he was not averse to plunking on purpose. He also fostered feuds, particularly with even more cantankerous Ty Cobb, who once bunted down the line so he could spike Mays when the pitcher covered first base.[1]

Indians veteran infielder Ray Chapman knew all about Mays's reputation, though he enjoyed little success against him. Chapman had faced the former Red Sox' two-time 20-game winner often during his own nine-year career. So when he stepped to the plate in the fifth inning with his team ahead 3–0, he might have indeed anticipated an unfriendly reception. After all, Mays had already yielded a home run and his butter-finger fielders had allowed two more Tribesmen to cross the plate.

Chapman crouched in his usual stance, crowding the plate. Mays released his first pitch—and the last pitch in the life of Ray Chapman. It hit him in the head with a sickening thud (batting helmets were not required at the time) and trickled toward the mound, where Mays, in the belief it struck bat, picked it up and fired to first. Chapman dropped to one knee with eyes closed and mouth open. Only onrushing Yankees catcher Muddy Ruel prevented him from collapsing to the ground. Home plate umpire Tommy Connolly called for a doctor, who tried to revive Chapman after he had lost consciousness. Chapman finally got on his feet but stumbled toward the clubhouse as his legs buckled and had to be carried off the field. Mays never moved from the mound. He merely asked for a new baseball.

Nearby St. Lawrence Hospital received Chapman, who faded in and out of consciousness and could not speak. He had sustained a depressed fracture more than three inches long on the left side of his skull. Doctors operated immediately, but the hour-long procedure in which a piece of his skull was removed revealed that his brain had been lacerated on both sides after striking the bone.

Optimism returned when his pulse and breathing improved. Player-manager Tris Speaker, who led a contingent of Indians to the hospital, informed Chapman's wife of the incident. She boarded a train to New York. But soon high hopes had melted into misery. Chapman died before the morning sun rose. His widow fainted upon hearing the tragic news from a Philadelphia priest and family friend who had traveled to the Big Apple to meet her.[2]

Friends of Mays claimed he was badly shaken upon hearing of Chapman's death. He did issue a remorseful statement to the district attorney and later stated it was the most regrettable incident of his career, one that he would "give anything to undo." But many felt that if any major league pitcher was destined to create such horror, it was Mays, who had been accused of scuffing baseballs to darken them and make them harder to see. It was believed that Chapman never caught a glimpse of the baseball that killed him. American League president Ban Johnson offered his prediction that Mays would never take the mound again. But not only did the submariner continue his career, he led the league with 27 victories the following season and pitched until 1929. He claimed that his snub from Hall of Fame voters was a direct result of the pitch that doomed Chapman.

The Indians were forced to move on without their friend and teammate. They dedicated their season to Chapman, but the tragedy made an immediate negative impact. They lost eight of their next eleven games and fell three and a half games out of first place on August 26, their largest deficit of the season. But they finished the year on a 24–8 run that included a seven-game winning streak that catapulted them into first place to stay. They had won their first pennant. The Brooklyn Robins awaited them in the World Series.[3]

Ironically, it had been Chapman's replacement at shortstop that helped catapult the Indians to the American League crown. Future Hall of Famer Joe Sewell was eventually summoned and provided a September spark. He batted .329 with a .413 on-base percentage to fill in more than admirably. Sewell would go on to register a .312 career average and finish among the top 20 in Most Valuable Player voting six times.[4]

Major League Baseball yearned for the attention created by the Cleveland-Brooklyn World Series. The Black Sox Scandal had recently broke as White Sox players admitted shamefully to throwing the previous Fall Classic, most famously and historically costing the career of Shoeless Joe Jackson. The Black Sox had given baseball a black eye. All involved hoped that an honest and competitive best-of-nine World Series in 1920 would be the first step to bringing the sport back to respectability.

The starting pitchers dominated early. Remarkably consistent Indians ace Stan Coveleski, who would eventually join Sewell in the Hall, hurled a five-hitter in Game 1 for a 3–1 victory and shackled Brooklyn again in Game 4. Those two performances sandwiched around Robins victories left the series tied at 2–2. The Tribe had scored just nine runs in the first four games. Game 5 would prove critical, but the Indians' bats were not exactly booming. They finally found their batting eyes and strokes in the first inning. Charlie Jamieson, Bill Wambsganss, and Tris Speaker reached base against tough right-hander Burleigh Grimes, who had blanked the Indians in Game 2. Up to the plate stepped Smith, who had gone hitless in four at-bats against Grimes in that game. Smith fruitlessly flailed away at two spitballs—a Grimes specialty. His next pitch was a fastball that caught the meat of the plate. Smith smashed the offering high over the right-field fence at Dunn Field (what League Park had been temporarily renamed) and onto Lexington Avenue. The no-doubter was the first grand slam in World Series history. The 26,884 raucous fans in attendance roared their approval. Smith spoke to the *Cleveland Press* following the game about his historic achievement and how the baserunners were depending on him to send them across the plate. His words dripped with days-long-gone baseball lexicon.

"I knew that these three lads on the sacks were pulling for me to deliver, while I couldn't help but feeling the excitement in the stands," he said. "That home-run pitch was just what the doctor ordered. I hit it as squarely on the nose as I ever hit any ball and I could feel it was destined to travel the way it cracked off my bat."[5]

Game 5 heroics were not limited to Smith and Bagby, who was in the process of shutting down the Robins and created a bit of history of his own when he hit a three-run homer to become the first pitcher to go deep in a World Series game. A more unlikely star would emerge in the comparatively nondescript Wambsganss, a decent batsman and solid second baseman who had admitted he had yet to recover emotionally from the death of Chapman, his friend and double-play partner. Wambsganss failed to hit safely in nine at-bats in the first three games of the series as Cleveland fans began to lose patience with him. Wambsganss admitted to *Baseball Magazine* editor F. C. Lane that he was still struggling with the loss of Chapman. But the 26-year-old infielder began showing signs of life by slamming two singles in Game 4.

Wambsganss took his momentum and ran with it in Game 5 when he singled and scored on the Smith blast. But it was not at the plate that he would etch his name into the history books. That moment in time occurred in the fifth inning after Bagby finally showed a crack in the armor as relievers started warming up in the bullpen. He allowed successive singles to Pete Kilduff and Otto Miller with a 7–0 advantage. That certainly represented no threat to the lead, but the fans at Dunn might have gotten a bit nervous had the Robins followed with any more hits. Clarence Mitchell, who had replaced Grimes on the mound, stepped to the plate as Brooklyn manager Wilbert Robinson eschewed the use of a pinch-hitter in the understanding that the hurler was also a decent hitter (he would conclude his career with a .252 lifetime batting average). Wambsganss played so deep in the hope of cutting off a hit that could score a run that he stepped into the outfield. Robinson boldly called for a hit-and-run. Mitchell slammed a liner toward center field, but Wambsganss, who had broken toward second base, snagged the ball to retire Mitchell. He touched the bag to eliminate Kilduff, then tagged Miller, who had stopped dead in his tracks.

Wambsganss had executed the second unassisted triple play in baseball history (Neal Ball of the Indians had pulled off the feat in 1909). It remains the only unassisted triple play in a World Series and one of just

15 ever accomplished.[6] "Just before I tagged [Miller], he said, 'Where'd you get that ball?'" recalled Wambsganss in an interview with *The Sporting News* in January 1966. "I said, 'Well, I've got it and you're out number three.'"[7]

The fans sat silent temporarily after the play as they tried to compute what had happened. Then they erupted in celebration. The Robins never regained a sense of momentum. Even though they slugged 13 hits off Bagby, they managed just one run in an 8–1 Indians victory. The series was not over—but it was over. Brooklyn did not score again. Tribe hurlers Duster Mails and Coveleski, who won all three starts, blanked the Robins in Games 6 and 7, respectively, to give the franchise its first world championship. But before it was over, Cleveland mayor Ed FitzGerald presented Smith and Wambsganss with diamond-studded medals for

Bill Wambsganss (top left) completes the only unassisted triple play in World Series history.

their Game 5 heroics. So inconsequential was the status of the latter in the world of baseball that the *Washington Post* reported that one of the keepsakes had been given to "Phil Wambsganss." Indeed, he finished the series batting just .154 after managing one measly infield hit in the last two games combined.[8]

But thousands of players with far greater credentials over a century of baseball that has since been played never received the notoriety given to Wambsganss, who stands alone in the history of the game as the only man ever to turn an unassisted triple play—indeed, be involved in any triple play—in a World Series.

CHAPTER FOUR

Revealing Rapid Robert

THE POPULATION OF VAN METER, IOWA, WAS ABOUT 400 IN 1936. NOT until the turn of the 21st century did it crawl over 1,000. The odds of the tiny farming community producing arguably the greatest right-handed pitcher ever were infinitesimal. Van Meter High School has never been described as a baseball factory. Yet one cannot deny history. And, indeed, Bob Feller did burst onto the scene as a major league phenom with the Cleveland Indians mere months after having emerged from the wheat fields of Van Meter.[1]

That might have come as a surprise to anyone but Bill Feller. Farmer Bill had designs on making his son a star. The man who worked 360 acres along the Raccoon River simply loved baseball and he yearned not only to instill that passion in Bob, but to provide him the tools to achieve greatness on the mound. He tossed a rubber ball to the boy before he could even walk, then would hold up a pillow to catch the return toss. Bill switched to growing wheat from corn because the former was easier to harvest, thereby giving his son more time to practice baseball. Never mind that his hand was hurting from working the farm—Bob always made time to pitch to his dad. He whet his appetite for pitching off a makeshift rubber toward two wooden slabs that served as home plate by listening to Chicago Cubs games on radio station WHO in Des Moines. The contests were broadcast by future president Ronald Reagan.

It did not take long for the young Feller to blossom. At age 11 in 1930, he pitched several games in battles between the Van Meter High School team and its elementary school counterpart. Feller could throw harder than any of the high school kids. Soon Bill and Bob took the momentous step of building a ballpark on the farm to provide opportunities for local players and to spotlight the kid's talent. They called the field Oakview Park and charged 25 cents admission. Games often attracted up to 1,000 fans. "Feller Field" boasted a small grandstand and scoreboard. Though Feller initially played shortstop, his dominance as a pitcher forced a switch. The move to the mound would prove to be permanent.[2]

Meanwhile, the cold Midwest winters were no problem. Bill and Bob played pitch-and-catch on the second story of the three-story barn. Or the younger Feller would simply fire fastballs into the door, which eventually needed to be replaced after having been pounded into oblivion.[3,4]

Feller would not be the secret of his dad much longer. He joined an American Legion team in nearby Adel and soon gained a reputation as a budding star. Feller was not the only future standout on the team—he hurled baseballs to future University of Iowa running back Nile Kinnick, who would become the only Heisman Trophy winner in school history and receive the posthumous honor (having been killed during World War II) of having its football stadium named after him.

Throngs of fans streamed in to watch Feller shut down foe after foe. So dominant was Feller that he led Adel into the state championship game. He also pitched for several other teams, include the one representing Van Meter High School, for whom he reportedly threw five no-hitters. Feller ascended to the semipro Farmers Union team in Des Moines during the summer of 1935, pitching against far tougher competition and in front of many major league scouts. The statistics kept by his father recorded 361 strikeouts in 157 innings with 42 hits allowed and an earned-run average under 1.00. Though such numbers seem implausible, that Feller dominated at that level remains undeniable.

Feller traveled with Farmers Union to Dayton in September 1935 for the national amateur tournament. Scouts drooled as he pitched a two-hitter and fanned 18 in a 1–0 defeat to Battle Creek. He was flooded with offers that included significant bonuses, but little did they know that he had already signed a deal with the Indians two months earlier. Cleveland scout and Iowa native Cy Slapnicka had found his way to a game pitched by Feller. Slapnicka sat uncomfortably on a car bumper and watched with growing awe and excitement a level of talent he had never previously witnessed.[5,6]

Slapnicka wasted no time inking Feller to a contract for $1 and an autographed baseball, though Bill was required to sign along with his underage son. The deal ostensibly intended to place the 17-year-old with Cleveland's minor league affiliate in Fargo, North Dakota, but it basically served to stash the flamethrower away from other major league teams. Slapnicka transferred the contract to the New Orleans Pelicans of the Southern Association, but tough-minded baseball commissioner Kenesaw Mountain Landis would not tolerate such shenanigans, voiding the deal. Bill threatened to take Major League Baseball to court, forcing Landis to relent. The younger Feller, who respected and adored Slapnicka and had come to embrace the Cleveland organization, immediately resigned with the Indians. He would never pitch for another team.[7]

The spotlight shone on Feller on July 6 when he debuted professionally in an exhibition game against the St. Louis Cardinals—the vaunted Gashouse Gang. Feller yielded just one unearned run in three innings and fanned eight, including standouts of the era Rip Collins, Pepper Martin, and Leo Durocher twice each. So impressed was Durocher that he blurted out to the umpire upon arriving at the plate for his second at-bat, "I feel like a clay pigeon in a shooting gallery." When asked to pose with Feller after the game, St. Louis superstar pitcher Dizzy Dean honored the 17-year-old phenom by stating that it should be Feller giving permission for the photo.[8]

Feller never pitched in a minor league game. He emerged from the bullpen to debut in Washington against the Senators on July 19, 1936, walking two and striking out one in a scoreless inning. He struggled with his control in relief over the next several weeks, as he would through much of his career. But when he was given the chance to make his first start against the woeful St. Louis Browns in Cleveland on August 23, he displayed the fastball that has been estimated at 100 miles per hour and enough accuracy to dominate. He pitched a complete-game six-hitter with four walks and 15 strikeouts to fall just one short of Rube Waddell's American League record.

Bob Feller exploded onto the scene as the greatest pitcher ever to wear a Cleveland uniform.

Three weeks later he wiped it out. Feller fanned 17 Philadelphia Athletics to tie the major league mark set by Dean. But he also walked nine in totaling a pitch count that would have had him removed from the mound by the fifth inning had he been active in the modern era. That he yielded just two runs speaks of the inability of opposing hitters to make consistent contact. Feller remained in the starting rotation that season from August 23 forward and lowered his ERA from a peak of 7.88 to 3.44 by the end of the year.

His dream had come true. Feller spoke years later about turning that dream into reality. "I never intended to be anything other than a ballplayer," he said. "Like Thomas Edison said, 'Find out something you like to do and you'll never have to work the rest of your life.' Well, I took his advice. That's exactly what I did."[9]

And he did it as well as any pitcher ever has. But he did not merely overpower batters with his fastball. He featured a crackling, fall-off-the-table curveball and high leg kick that intimated hitters. Feller was the most overpowering pitcher that any major league had seen since Walter Johnson. His talents grew to such legendary status that they were featured in 1940s newsreels proving that his fastball traveled faster than a motorcycle. So popular had Feller become that he was featured on postseason barnstorming tours against African American players and matched up against Negro League legend Satchel Paige. Yet the outspoken Feller did his legacy no favors later in his career when he questioned the major league credentials of Jackie Robinson (claiming he had "football shoulders" and could not hit a curve) and stated years thereafter that his career made a greater impact on the sport than that of the man who broke the color barrier.[10,11]

At an age when most players were still honing their skills at the high school and college levels or deep in the minors—he returned to Van Meter for his graduation *after* his major league debut—Feller required a few seasons to harness his control. He set a dubious modern-day record that still stands with 208 walks in 1938 and led the American League in that department in two of the next three years. But he was also in the process of pacing the circuit in strikeouts for seven consecutive full seasons and his wildness did not prevent him from compiling a 76–33 record from 1939 to 1941 and leading the league in earned run average in 1940. That was the year he crafted the only Opening Day no-hitter in baseball history, blanking the White Sox, 1–0.

Feller was also deeply patriotic. While others awaited their draft notices following the Japanese attack on Pearl Harbor, he became the first professional American athlete to enlist. He joined the US Navy two days later and earned eight battle stars as chief of a gun crew on the battleship USS *Alabama*. Though he had received a military exemption due to his dad's failing health, he yearned to serve in combat missions rather than becoming a showpiece to maintain morale in the military, as other athletes had done. "I told them I wanted to . . . get into combat, wanted to do something besides standing around handing out balls and bats and making ball fields out of coral reefs," Feller explained.[12]

Indians fans that feared his skills would deteriorate due to inaction were greatly relieved when he returned late in 1945 and began pitching better than ever. Feller enjoyed his finest season in 1946, winning 26 games and sporting a career-low 2.18 ERA. His 348 strikeouts established a major league mark that remained unbroken until Sandy Koufax shattered it in 1965. And his 36 complete games remain atop the list and might stay there forever given the nature of the sport in the 21st century.

What Feller could not accomplish was a postseason victory. His only opportunity occurred when the Indians finally upended the Yankees and secured the 1948 American League pennant with the first playoff win in baseball history, an 8–3 triumph against the host Red Sox. Feller, whose ERA rose nearly a point that year and strikeouts dropped markedly, was sharp in Game 1 of the World Series against Boston's National League team. He blanked the Braves for seven innings of a scoreless tie before allowing a leadoff walk to Bill Salkeld in the eighth. Pinch-runner Phil Masi was sacrificed to second, then apparently picked off by Feller at second. But umpire Bill Stewart blew the call and Masi scored on a single by Tommy Holmes in a 1–0 Indians defeat. Masi admitted in his will that he was out.[13] Feller was clobbered in Game 5, thereby sustaining the only two defeats the Indians suffered in their last World Series triumph. His decline was already nearly complete when he was bypassed as a fifth starter throughout the 1954 World Series sweep at the hands of the Giants.

Feller finally ended his career in 1956. He likely would have won 350 games had he not lost four years of his prime to World War II. And though Addie Joss compiled superior single-season statistics and Corey Kluber earned two Cy Young Awards and counting in the second decade of the 21st century, there has been little argument that the length and brilliance of his career makes Feller the greatest Indians pitcher of all time. That sentiment was certainly shared by American League hitters, including none other than the immortal Ted Williams, who stated that Feller was the "fastest and best pitcher I ever saw in my career." Few of his peers would have argued.[14]

CHAPTER FIVE

The Cleveland Crybabies

AMONG THE USUAL ATTRIBUTES OF CONTENDING TEAMS IN MAJOR League Baseball is camaraderie, a sense of togetherness and purpose. Such is not always the case. The early 1970s Oakland Athletics battled not only opponents on the field, but each other off it. And they won three consecutive World Series titles.

The 1940 Indians certainly fell into that category. But their beef was not with teammates. Rather, it was a hatred for manager Oscar Vitt. And though one can only speculate how that loathing affected their play on the field, one can certainly claim—considering they finished just one game behind Detroit for the American League pennant—that it might have cost them a second crown.

The seeds of discontent were planted shortly after Indians principal owner Alva Bradley hired Vitt before the 1938 season. He had been managing the Newark Bears in the Yankees organization, but jumped at the opportunity to take over a big-league club. Cleveland players eventually wished he had jumped elsewhere—they might have requested he go jump in the lake. But the soap opera that followed seemed typical of an Indians organization that had become greatly criticized for its malfunctions and questionable practices by the late 1930s. "If there were an Alcatraz in baseball, the Cleveland club would certainly qualify," offered Shirley Povich of the *Washington Post*. "Their faculty for getting into trouble is no less than amazing."

Legendary sportswriter Grantland Rice believed Vitt was walking into a hornet's nest. "Oscar Vitt starts in Cleveland, where some good men have failed," Rice wrote on the eve of the 1938 season. "Cleveland's baseball temperament is unstable. The hopes of the fans are riding high one day and coasting to the depths the next. And too frequently the manager has been caught in the middle. Sharply critical scribes, noisily articulate fans, and, too frequently ballplayers who huddled in cliques in the clubhouse corners, have wrecked the careers of managers who have tried desperately to win in Cleveland." Rice added his admiration for Vitt, whom he praised for accepting the managerial post without hesitation despite knowledge of imminent danger.[1]

Vitt received similar commendation in 1938, when despite his no-nonsense approach that resulted in a suspension threat of boozing and abusive catcher Rollie Hemsley and fine of star pitcher Johnny Allen for allowing the sleeve on his uniform to become ragged, he guided the team to a third-place finish. Though player discontent has been speculated, it was not until 1939 that his disciplinary zeal resulted in what one newspaper claimed to be a "smoldering rebellion against the manager by some members of the team." The Indians were hanging only around .500 and rumors of ownership discontent surfaced, but Bradley responded by signing Vitt to a new contract, stating that the players needed to know who was in charge and that they better get used to it, for their manager was destined to return the following year. The team responded by finishing on a 29–13 run and a fine record of 87–57.[2]

All involved were soon to learn that greatness and solidarity are not mutually exclusive, though the 1940 season began swimmingly. Biases apparently not aside, Cleveland sportswriters picked the Indians to win the pennant. Hemsley announced he had given up drinking, thanks to Alcoholics Anonymous. Emerging ace Bob Feller crafted what remains the only Opening Day no-hitter in baseball history when he blanked the host White Sox. The team won 14 of its first 20 games to firmly establish its status as a contender along with Boston and Detroit that would remain strong throughout the season.

But Vitt's abrasive personality and combative relationship with his players began to bubble beyond the surface. He complained publicly about issues the players believed should have been discussed behind clubhouse doors. He ranted after errors on the field. Players believed he

Manager Oscar Vitt nearly won a pennant in 1940 despite being despised by his players.
COURTESY OF THE CLEVELAND MEMORY PROJECT

would lambast them behind their backs to fellow managers, opposing players, and reporters. Some in the media called for his firing. Others lauded his toughness and intolerance of mistakes. Blunders on the field inspired tirades.[3]

Vitt exhibited no restraint toward even his finest talent. He fumed in the dugout as Feller struggled in a June outing against the Red Sox, asking his players in the dugout and within earshot of the young phenom how the Indians could possibly win a pennant with him as the ace of the staff. A day later he ranted similarly about veteran pitcher and future Hall of Famer Mel Harder after another defeat to Boston. "When are you going to start earning your salary?" he screamed. "It's about time you won one, the money you're getting." Harder, who was unceremoniously banished from the mound in the first inning, yelled back that he was doing the best he could.[4]

Indeed, Harder had raised his earned run average to a disturbing 7.33 with that performance, but Vitt's invectives motivated the players to act. A group that included Harder and premier slugger Hal Trosky pulled aside *Cleveland Press* beat writer Frank Gibbons. Requesting to keep their words off the record, Trosky asked, "We're going to get rid of Vitt and we wonder what you think of it?" In the knowledge that such a rebellion would certainly find its way into the papers, Gibbons replied that such a move would backfire and make the players appear childish while having the opposite effect on Vitt's status. After all, the team had stayed in contention for its first pennant in 20 years.[5]

Gibbons's warning did not prevent the players from lodging a protest to Bradley in a show of either force or petulance (depending on viewpoint) that the Associated Press termed "unprecedented in major league baseball history." They claimed they could not win under Vitt, yet they remained on the doorstep of first place. Bradley, however, gave the protest merit, especially considering the highly respected Feller was among the players in his office. Bradley warned them to maintain secrecy to the media, but reporters learned of the mutiny and lined up on both sides. An apparent leak among the players (future Hall of Fame shortstop Lou Boudreau stated years later that he believed it to be Hemsley, but others speculated it was Harder) resulted in legendary Cleveland sportswriter Gordon Cobbledick quickly getting the story and contacting Bradley, who was forced to admit its truth. Cobbledick backed the rebellion, citing the charges of players that they could not hustle for Vitt and that their spirits had been crushed. He wrote that the complaints proved that Vitt was a poor manager. But Cleveland fans did not agree. They cheered Vitt and booed the players upon their return from Boston.

The negative reaction and media publicity caused all the Indians in attendance at a meeting to sign a statement that withdrew their protest.[6] Such an attempt to save face did not placate the distressed and angered Vitt, nor the media, which labeled the players as sneaky. The Indians were soon known as the Cleveland Crybabies. They were also labeled a "bawl team" and "Half-Vitts."[7]

Vitt voiced particular disappointment about the involvement of Feller, who, he claimed was like a son to him. In 1956, upon his retirement, Feller admitted that he hated Vitt's guts and did not mind telling the world. Bradley later claimed that if he had fired Vitt in June and replaced him with popular coach Luke Sewell, the Indians might have won the pennant by 20 games. But he added that such a move would have allowed players throughout the game to believe they had power over their managers. Bradley believed creating such a precedent would damage the sport. He concluded that Vitt would have to remain in charge the rest of the season.[8]

Through it all, the Indians continued to win. In fact, they sizzled after the story broke, winning 12 of 15 during a tremendous homestand to vault into first place. They stayed either atop the standings or within one and a half games of the lead into mid-August, then remained in first until September 6, stretching their advantage to as many as five and a half games. Bradley, however, understood that the die had been cast. He admitted in August that not even a World Series championship could repair the relationship between Vitt and his players.

Baseball fans proved merciless. While *The Sporting News* launched a campaign to ban soda pop bottles from ballparks, where they could be hurled at unsuspecting players, patrons began tossing baby bottles at the Indians. The unnerved Tribe lost six straight in early September, then recovered as a neck-and-neck battle against Detroit ensued. The team arrived via train on September 19 for a three-game series against the Tigers in Motor City, where fans pelted them with eggs and tomatoes. The players required a police escort to reach their hotel, but the harassment continued as they were serenaded by fans playing musical instruments on the sidewalk. When the Indians arrived at the ballpark the following day, their dugout had been decorated with diapers while fans wheeled baby carriages onto its roof. The Indians lost the first two games of the set before recovering to win the third.[9]

It was the first of those defeats that proved most emotionally devastating. Harder shackled Detroit on three hits through seven with his team leading 4–1. He allowed a walk and a single, prompting Vitt to replace him with Feller, who had been overworked as both a starter and reliever. "Rapid Robert" was too tired to be rapid. He allowed three straight hits to blow the lead and the game. The Indians had fallen out of first place for good.

The fruit really hit the fan—or, rather, the fans really threw the fruit—when the Tigers repaid the visit a week later for a season-ending series. The Indians needed a sweep to capture the pennant and their fans were ready for revenge. The patrons arrived at the park with baskets of fruits and vegetables to throw at the Tigers. Even the most pristine women among a tremendous Ladies Day crowd of 45,553 launched fresh produce. Detroit superstar Hank Greenberg was nailed with a tomato as he chased after a fly ball in the outfield. As the public address announcer informed the fans that a forfeit was imminent, thereby killing any chance at a championship, and police fanned out to catch offenders, a young Cleveland fan named Armen Guerra unloaded a tomato crate from the upper deck that knocked out Tigers catcher Birdie Tebbetts. Guerra was captured and escorted to the Detroit clubhouse, where a revived Tebbetts gave him a much-deserved pounding. Guerra responded by charging the backstop with criminal assault. Making matters worse, the Tigers blanked Feller and the Tribe to clinch the pennant.[10]

There would be no drama to conclude this soap opera. The ouster of Vitt seemed inevitable and, indeed, he was fired after what he described as a "nightmarish" season, though he claimed that only a few ringleaders had convinced others to join the revolt because upper management had not backed him with enough fervor. General manager Cy Slapnicka, who had discovered and signed Feller, soon resigned. A seething Vitt, who believed he had been betrayed, expressed his deepest sympathy for managerial replacement Roger Peckinpaugh, who lasted just one year and experienced some of the same issues with Indians players, though they were neither as pronounced nor as publicized. It was not until Boudreau assumed the position as a young player-manager that contentment reigned. But, oddly, Vitt had managed the Indians to their three best records since 1932 and their top marks until 1948, when Boudreau guided them to their second American League title and last World Series championship.

The sands of time have left blame for the Crybabies debacle up for interpretation. The immediate reaction was one of derision on both sides. During an offseason baseball writers' dinner in New York, a skit portrayed Indians players in the army complaining to Bradley that they were being mistreated. Their grievances were followed by "Sergeant Vitt" arriving on the scene with a bullwhip. The season was over, but the 1940 Indians would go down as one of the most dysfunctional bunches in baseball history.[11]

CHAPTER SIX

The Jackie Robinsons
of the American League

A 500-POUND MAN PLUNGING FROM A DIVING BOARD IN A CANNONBALL could not have made a bigger splash than Jackie Robinson in 1947. In comparison, the dive taken by Larry Doby and the Indians later that year barely created a ripple. Unfortunately, Doby has received little credit historically for his courage in enduring inevitable racism as he integrated the American League, just as Robinson did the National League. Moreover, the Indians made two bold moves in helping break the shameful color barrier that had prevented the sport from living up to its claim that is was truly America's pastime. They also signed Satchel Paige in 1948 as the first black pitcher in the major leagues.

Doby, in one aspect of his journey, had it tougher than Robinson. After all, the latter experienced one year in the minor leagues to adapt to life as the lone African American on a team. He was also nearly five years older than Doby with a toughness and maturity far beyond even those years. Doby was plucked by daring Indians owner Bill Veeck straight out of the Negro Leagues. He was signed on the eve of Independence Day and used as a pinch-hitter on July 5 at Comiskey Park in Chicago. Doby was forced to overcome other barriers. Though he eventually proved himself worthy of Hall of Fame induction, he was less athletically gifted than Robinson and, in fact, struggled mightily in his first season with Cleveland. He simply could not outplay the racist taunts as the first black player against whom American League rivals competed. The worthiness of Robinson became evident almost immediately. That of Doby would have to wait one torturous year.

The seeds of the relationship between Doby and the Indians were planted long before the 1946 season that Robinson spent with Triple-A Montreal. Veeck had been eager to integrate baseball since some players began packing their duffle bags for overseas following the Japanese bombing of Pearl Harbor. That was when he requested that Harlem Globetrotters promoter Abe Saperstein prepare a list of premier black baseball prospects. Veeck, whose progressive racial beliefs had been influenced by his father, a former owner of the Chicago Cubs, had planned to buy and integrate the Philadelphia Athletics. But his purchase was nixed by Commissioner Kennesaw Mountain Landis.[1]

In 1946, when Veeck had landed the job as president of the Indians, he hired an African American named Louis Jones to prepare Cleveland's black community for the integration of the Indians. Jones toiled in public relations for the American Federation of Labor and later married famed entertainer Lena Horne. Veeck then sent veteran scout and minor league manager "Reindeer Bill" Killefer on what amounted to a secret mission. Killefer was to find young Negro League talent without revealing the grand plan. Veeck did not consult Indians manager Lou Boudreau, but he did pick the brain of sportswriter Wendell Smith of the black weekly *Pittsburgh Courier*. The brain trust then put their heads together and decided that Doby was their man.[2]

A fellow African American newspaper reporter with the appropriate and highly coincidental name of Cleveland Jackson, who wrote for the *Cleveland Call and Post*, caught wind of the story. He confirmed it with Veeck and ran a piece on June 28 that the Indians were indeed considering signing Doby. A last-minute check into Doby's character by Jones confirmed the positivity that Veeck already suspected. He didn't even drink, smoke, or swear.

That bit of news clinched it. Veeck offered Eagles owners Abe and Effa Manley $5,000 more if they kept Doby. Manley not only accepted the deal, but in a gesture that proved their desire to provide opportunities for the players to continue integrating Major League Baseball, also offered to hand over fellow outfielder Monte Irvin for practically nothing. In what would prove to be a monumental mistake, Veeck turned down the chance to grab the future Hall of Famer.[3]

Doby had batted .322 for the Eagles in 1946. Further intriguing was that he had helped his team win the Negro League championship by defeating Paige and the Kansas City Monarchs in its World Series. He continued to play for the Eagles early in 1947 and homered in his last at-bat for the team. Veeck purchased his contract with little fanfare and wasted no time having him don an Indians uniform. The sight was not a pretty one as he entered the Comiskey Park clubhouse for the first time to meet with Boudreau. His new teammates refused to look at him or speak with him. The cold shoulder upset Doby, as one might expect. It was not his idea of comradeship. "I knew it was segregated times, but I had never seen anything like that in athletics," he said in 2002. "I was embarrassed. It was tough." Doby was forced to visit the Chicago clubhouse to borrow a first baseman's glove because none of the Indians players offered him one.[4]

Boudreau had issued a statement explaining to the world that his team had signed Doby and that it should represent nothing more than a typical purchase despite its historical significance. "The acquisition of Larry Doby, an infielder formerly with the Newark Eagles team, is a routine baseball purchase in my mind," the statement read. "Creed, race or color are not factors in baseball success, whether it be in the major or minor leagues. Ability and character are the only factors."[5]

Doby had plenty of both, though his ability was far slower to become evident than it was for Robinson, who was on his way to winning National League Rookie of the Year honors. Doby fanned in his first at-bat on July 5, singled for his first major league hit the next day, then played sparingly the rest of the year, finishing with a meager .156 batting average. Only that significant time on the bench prevented him from receiving the same level of racist taunting that Robinson was forced to endure. But Veeck certainly read what Doby didn't hear. Though the Cleveland fans generally welcomed the newcomer, Veeck reported in his autobiography that he received more than 20,000 letters, most of which were obscene or threatened violence. Veeck painstakingly answered all of them.[6]

Boudreau refused to allow Doby's struggles to affect his plans for 1948. He recognized talent. He moved Doby from the infield to the outfield, where he remained for the rest of his career. Boudreau stuck with Doby despite a mediocre first half of a season in which the team established itself as a pennant contender. And he was rewarded when Doby caught fire down the stretch. He hit safely in 39 of 43 games from August 14 to the end of the regular season, batting .358 (57 for 159) during a period that included a 20-game hitting streak. He raised his mark to .301 at year's end and slammed two doubles in the epic playoff game against the host Red Sox that gave the Indians their first pennant in 28 years.

By that time, Veeck had made another bold move that further integrated baseball and saved the sport from the historical embarrassment of never featuring arguably the greatest pitcher in history. That Satchel Paige spent two decades disallowed from proving his brilliance on the mound is embarrassment enough. And when Veeck indeed signed Paige on July 7, the media reacted with greater criticism than when he brought Doby aboard. Those who speculated that Paige was as old as 50 believed it to be no more than a publicity stunt. Among those who expressed such an opinion was J. G. Taylor Spink, publisher of the baseball bible known as *The Sporting News*, who wrote the following:

> *In criticizing the acquisition of Satchel Paige by Cleveland, THE SPORTING NEWS believes that Veeck has gone too far in his quest of publicity, and that he has done his league's position absolutely no good insofar as public reaction is concerned . . . Paige said he was 39 years of ago [sic]. There are reports that he is somewhere in the neighborhood of 50. It would have done Cleveland and the American League no good in the court of public opinion if, at 50, Paige were as Caucasian as, let us say, Bob Feller. To bring in a pitching "rookie" of Paige's age casts a reflection on the entire scheme of operation in the major leagues. To sign a hurler at Paige's age is to demean the standards of baseball in the big circuits. Further complicating the situation is that suspicion that if Satchel were white, he would not have drawn a second thought from Veeck.* [7]

It seemed nobody but Paige—least of all Spink—knew exactly how old the tall, lanky right-hander was at the time. He was 42, and definitely not done. He blanked the St. Louis Browns over two innings in his first appearance with the Indians on July 9, earned his first major league victory in his next outing, and continued to sparkle in relief. He defeated the Washington Senators in his first start on August 3 before a home crowd of 72,434, then stunned the baseball world 10 days later by shutting out the Chicago White Sox on five hits in Comiskey. The best was yet to come. Paige tossed a three-hit shutout on August 20 against the same Sox for a taut 1–0 victory before a near-sellout crowd of 78,382 at Cleveland Stadium to lower his ERA to 1.33 and extend his shutout streak to 24⅔ innings. The successive shutouts inspired Veeck to dispatch a telegram to Spink that read, "Paige pitching—no runs, three hits. Definitely in line for the Sporting News Rookie of the Year Award. Regards, Bill Veeck."[8]

He continued to pitch both as a starter and a reliever—a common practice for hurlers through the 1960s—tossing a complete game victory over Washington on August 30 to run his season-ending record to 6–1. Despite a September swoon he finished the year with a 2.48 ERA and just two home runs allowed in 72⅔ innings. He baffled the opposition with a variety of windups, arm angles, and pitches.

Paige hurled just one scoreless inning in the World Series. But Doby played the role of hero. He batted .318 in the six-game defeat of the Boston Braves and slammed the decisive home run in a pivotal Game 4 that placed his team on the precipice of the world championship. Of greater historical significance as the nation struggled to live up to its promise of racial harmony, he was hugged by winning pitcher Steve Gromek and that embrace was photographed for the world to see. The picture of the two beaming faces—one white, one black—remains one of the most iconic in the history of American sport. "That picture went out all over the country," Doby recalled during a 1987 interview with the *New York Times*. "I think it was one of the first, if not the first, of a black guy and white guy hugging, just happy because they won a ballgame."[9]

Doby emerged as one of the premier sluggers in the sport. He earned a spot on the All-Star team every season from 1949 to 1955, led

The immortal Satchel Paige warms up under the watchful eye of Indians owner Bill Veeck.

Satchel Paige & Bob Feller

The headline in this photo of Satchel Paige and Bob Feller says it all.

the circuit in home runs in 1952 and 1954, and finished second in the Most Valuable Player voting in the latter of those years. Many consider it absurd, especially given the emotional and mental hurdles Doby was forced to clear as the first African American player in the American League, that his Hall of Fame entry required a vote from the Veterans Committee nearly four decades after he retired. But the Indians recognized his legacy when they erected a statue of Doby outside Progressive Field in 2015.

The legend of Paige far exceeded that of his Cleveland counterpart, due to his greater ebullience and continued brilliance on the mound well into his 40s, which created a more lasting legacy. Paige pitched well for the Indians in 1949 before serving mostly as a late-inning reliever for the Browns the next three seasons. And in what was basically a publicity stunt in 1965, he showed he still had his stuff at age 60 when he blanked the Red Sox for three innings in a start for the Kansas City Athletics.

The Indians remained a forerunner for racial progress when they hired Frank Robinson as the first black manager in the major leagues in 1975. But it was the courage of men such as Veeck and Doby that paved the path for uninterrupted integration and truly made America's pastime a sport for all Americans.

CHAPTER SEVEN

The Greatest Triumph

THERE WERE OTHER YEARS, OTHER CHAMPIONSHIPS, ALBEIT NOT MANY. There was the 1920 World Series title. There were the bashers of the 1990s that won two pennants. There was the 2016 team that played its way to the precipice of winning it all. But none of those teams came closer to capturing the hearts and minds of Cleveland fans than the Indians of 1948.

The familiar and beloved voices of Jack Graney and Jimmy Dudley could be heard from porches around the city as radios blared broadcasts of games down the stretch run. Paying closer attention than ever were black Clevelanders who were buoyed by the signings of Larry Doby and Satchel Paige. More than 2.6 million fans streamed into Cleveland Stadium to watch their heroes, nearly doubling their previous record total set a year earlier and establishing an attendance mark that remained until 1995, after the team had moved to Jacobs Field.

The 1948 Indians did more than just win their second World Series crown. They launched an era of consistent contention in the American League that lasted a decade and resulted mostly in the frustrating and futile pursuit of the New York Yankees. But in that year, it was the Yankees doing all the chasing and not spending one day in first place. Though they remained close throughout, it was the Red Sox that battled the Indians tooth and nail for the pennant in the final months.

All the stars aligned that season. Though shortstop and player-manager Lou Boudreau had previously hit well for average and led the league three times in doubles, he emerged as a power hitter in 1948 and established career bests in batting, home runs, runs batted in, and runs scored in earning his only Most Valuable Player award. Third baseman Ken Keltner, whose numbers had fallen since losing 1945 to military service, rebounded to reach a peak in runs, home runs, and RBI. Second baseman Joe Gordon managed the last great year in a Hall of Fame career, finishing sixth in the MVP voting. But the shocking, stunning, shining star was rookie knuckleballer Gene Bearden, who won 20 of 27 decisions and led the league with a 2.43 ERA before fading into obscurity as one of the most storied one-hit wonders in baseball history. It was the offense, however, that carried the day, outscoring opponents by 272 on the year, the largest margin in Major League Baseball until the 1998 Yankees.[1]

Contributions came from many. But Boudreau was the undisputed leader—and not simply due to his managerial status. Boudreau was merely 30 years old but had served as a player-manager for seven years. His battered knees made him the slowest player in the American League, yet he continued to leg out doubles and show enough plate discipline to strike out just nine times all year. That Boudreau even remained an Indian in 1948 proved surprising. "Boy Owner" Bill Veeck, who was all of 32 at the time, planned on trading him to the lowly St. Louis Browns following the 1947 season, but the fans rebelled at the notion of losing their idol. "Sure, I tried to trade the guy off," Veeck later admitted. "So Boudreau made up his mind to make me look like a jerk. That's just what he did."[2]

Boudreau indeed pulled all the right strings. He utilized the young Doby and ancient Paige judiciously in maximizing their contributions. And, in one of the most courageous and instinctive moves ever made by a big-league manager, he bypassed veteran aces Bob Feller and Bob Lemon to select Bearden as the starting pitcher against the Red Sox in the first playoff game in major league history after the two teams finished in a tie at the top.

The Tribe almost didn't get there. They bolted to a hot start, but so did the surprising Philadelphia Athletics and their 81-year-old manager Connie Mack, who was born during the Civil War and had overseen the team since 1901. The Indians remained atop the standings or tied for the lead from June 5 to July 22, but never separated themselves from the pack

Bill Veeck and Lou Boudreau wave to fans at the parade celebrating the 1948 World Series title.

COURTESY OF THE CLEVELAND MEMORY PROJECT

by more than three and a half games. They ran hot and cold the rest of the way. A torrid stretch against the patsies of the American League in early August bumped their advantage to three games, but they lost 11 of 18 to fall into third place, four and a half games behind the sizzling Sox. The Indians then won 11 of 12 to surge to the top. Included was a critical defeat of Boston behind Feller that placed them in a flat-footed tie. The Indians could have clinched the pennant on the last day of the regular season, but Detroit ace Hal Newhouser beat Feller to force the playoff against the Red Sox the next afternoon.

Boudreau gathered his charges in the clubhouse after the defeat. He expressed his belief that the rookie Bearden was the hottest pitcher on the team and should start in Boston. But he allowed his players to chime in with their opinions and feelings. After all, he could still start the well-rested Lemon or Feller, who had tossed only two and a third innings that day. The players boasted unshakable confidence in their manager. "Joe Gordon popped up," recalled backup outfielder Bob Kennedy, "and said to Lou, 'We followed you this far and look where we are. There's no sense in changing anything now.' So everybody said, 'Okay, Bearden's it, let's go.'"[3]

The Red Sox would not know that Bearden was it. Boudreau yearned to keep it a secret, so he did not name his starter as the players traveled 12 hours by sleeper-car train to Boston. The Indians were surly as they got to Fenway Park—they could not flag down cabs from the train station to the hotel, so they had to drag their bags eight blocks and were still complaining upon their arrival at the storied venue. They spoke about taking out their anger on the pitches hurled to the plate. Then the game of cat and mouse continued. Asked by reporters to name his starting pitcher, Boudreau listed Feller, Lemon, and Bearden. The cat remained in the bag. All three told Red Sox clubhouse boys that they were pitching.

Bearden did not represent the only surprise managerial decision that day. Boston manager Joe McCarthy shocked and disappointed his players by bypassing ace Mel Parnell in favor of veteran right-hander Danny Galehouse, who had managed a mediocre 8–8 record that year. McCarthy believed the wind that day would hinder the left-handed Parnell. While the Indians embraced Boudreau's selection of his southpaw in a show of confidence, the Sox questioned that of their manager. The spirits of the Indians soared upon learning that they would be swinging their bats against Galehouse. The Red Sox, meanwhile, were shocked when gaining the same knowledge. Players later admitted that the news had a negative effect on them.[4]

Bearden lacked control, allowing a run in the first to negate Boudreau's solo blast in the top of the inning and requiring double plays to remain unscathed in the second, fourth, and seventh innings. The decisions of both managers appeared sound after the game remained tied at 1–1 through three. But singles by Boudreau and Gordon to open the fourth were followed by a towering Keltner homer onto the screen atop the Green Monster that chased Galehouse. The Indians grabbed the momentum and ran with it. Boudreau homered again and finished the

Gene Bearden is carried off the field after beating Boston to pitch the Tribe to the 1948 pennant.

game 4-for-4 while Bearden overcame a two-run homer by Bobby Doerr in the sixth as the Indians secured a spot in the World Series against the crosstown Boston Braves with an 8–3 victory. Bearden, meanwhile, had the Sox flailing away at knuckle curves off the plate. He claimed he didn't even realize it was the ninth inning when he tossed his last pitch, after which he was hoisted upon the shoulders of his teammates and carried off the field in celebration. The photo of the event remains among the most famous in Indians lore.

The Fall Classic that followed feels, at least historically, a bit anticlimactic. The taut 1–0 defeat to the Braves in Game 1 gained legend not for the pitching battle between Feller and fellow Hall of Famer Johnny Sain, but for perhaps the most famous missed call ever. Braves pinch-runner Phil Masi took his lead off second base in the eighth inning of the scoreless game. Feller wheeled around and fired a strike to Boudreau, who slapped the tag on Masi well before the latter reached his hand on the bag. But umpire Bill Stewart called Masi safe, setting off a heated argument. Nearly seven decades before the advent of replay challenges, Masi remained planted until Tommy Holmes scored him on a single that proved to be the only run of the game.

"We caught Masi napping," Feller wrote years later. "Unfortunately, we caught Bill Stewart of the National League doing the same things. Lou put the tag on Masi as he slid back into the bag. Neither the Braves nor Stewart knew we had that play in our book, so nobody was looking for it. . . . Lou tagged Masi out by two feet. It wasn't even close. Everybody in the ballpark saw Masi was out—except one—the umpire. We hadn't just picked off Masi. We had picked off Stewart too."[5]

According to *Chicago Sun-Times* sportswriter Raymond R. Coffey, Masi refused to talk about the play while Stewart remained alive. But Masi later admitted that he should have been called out. He then left no doubt when he acknowledged the same in his will. Feller continued to talk about it for good reason. After all, it might have cost him the only World Series triumph of his career. But Feller cannot be completely absolved. He started again in Game 5 and suffered a beating by Boston bats.

The Feller defeats were all the Braves could muster as the Indians secured their second championship. Lemon, Bearden, and Steve Gromek

GRANEY-CLEVELAND-AMER.

Former Tribe outfielder Jack Graney thrived years later as an Indians radio announcer.

allowed just five runs total in the other four games combined. Three of their efforts were complete games. Bearden relieved Lemon in the eighth inning of Game 6 and allowed two inherited runs to score as Boston closed the gap to 4–3, but the rookie knuckleballer blanked the Sox in the ninth to clinch the series. This time he was half-carried, half-dragged off the field as the Indians celebrated what they had not accomplished in 28 years.

The Indians arrived back in Cleveland via train and climbed into a dozen convertibles that rolled from the Cleveland Union Terminal to University Circle as an adoring crowd estimated at between 200,000 and 500,000 expressed thanks and joy.[6]

That joy would remain with them throughout their lives, but memories faded as year after year followed without a pennant. The majority of fans who attended the parade would not live to see the Indians win another American League championship. The team finished with a strong 89–65 record in 1949, but placed eight games behind the Yankees, who had regained their customary spot atop the standings. And later that year, a divorce settlement motivated Veeck to sell the team, but not before he buried the 1948 pennant in the outfield at Cleveland Stadium during a mock funeral.[7]

Memories have indeed faded. Few remain that can recall the excitement and passion they felt for the Tribe that year. But the team established far more than a footnote in history. The 1948 Indians achieved what even the dominant teams of the 1990s could not. They won it all while winning a place in the hearts and minds of Cleveland fans forever.

CHAPTER EIGHT

The Mistimed Slump

IT CAN BE CHILLY IN CLEVELAND FOR THE WORLD SERIES. JUST ASK THE 1995 Indians and their fans, who gladly braved snowy and bitter conditions to attend Game 3 at Jacobs Field, the first home Fall Classic contest in 41 years. They were freezing.

The 1954 Indians were also cold during the World Series. But it had nothing to with the climate along the lake. The temperatures in the two games played in their hometown were 80 and 84 degrees, respectively. No, they were literally warm. They were just figuratively cold, as in their bats, in the most unlikely four-game sweep in the history of the event.[1]

Though some consider the 1995 mashers that cruised to a 100–44 record the best Indians regular-season team of all time, the 1954 group that set an American League record with a 111–43 mark likely holds that distinction. They appeared flawless heading into the championship series in which they were heavily favored against the New York Giants. They boasted four of the top six vote-getters in the Most Valuable Player balloting in center fielder Larry Doby (league-leading 32 home runs and 124 runs batted in), second baseman Bobby Avila (.341 batting average), and starting pitchers Bob Lemon and Early Wynn, both of whom won 23 games. Seemingly forgotten by the voters were third baseman Al Rosen and pitcher Mike Garcia. The former drove in 102 runs and led the team with a .404 on-base percentage and .506 slugging percentage. The latter won 19 of 27 decisions and paced Cleveland starters with a 2.64 earned run average. The Indians easily led the American League with a 2.78 team ERA.

One might blame their World Series collapse on their regular-season dominance. The competitive fire of a team can be doused by a runaway pennant, but any team worth its salt should have no problem regaining its intensity for a run at the ultimate championship. And despite winning 111 games, the Indians did not shake the vaunted Yankees until late September. The Bronx Bombers managed their typical season, winning 103 games, and, after taking two of three from Cleveland in early September, remained just three and a half games out of first place.

The Yankees were still hanging around as they headed to Municipal Stadium for a doubleheader on September 12. A crowd of 86,563, which will forever remain the record attendance for a single game in franchise history, barring the construction of another huge stadium, jammed the park to watch their beloved team put their hated rivals away. The fans left with a joyful spirit after Lemon pitched a complete-game six-hitter in the opener for a 4–1 victory and Wynn struck out 12 in a 3–2 victory in the nightcap. The critical hit in Game 2 came from an unlikely source in reserve Wally Westlake, whose two-run double in the fifth inning gave the Tribe the lead for good.

The Indians had already gathered plenty of momentum as the World Series approached. Their sweep of New York was part of an 11-game winning streak that clinched the pennant. But they lost three of their last five regular-season games. One can only speculate whether that placed a cold compress on a hot team. Indians manager Al Lopez gave his starting position players significant rest down the stretch, which might have hurt their timing at the plate. Such a possibility can be debated, but never proven.

Not that the bats seemed to be coming out of cold storage at the start of Game 1 at the Polo Grounds—at least not that of sizzling first baseman Vic Wertz. Those among the majority that predicted doom for the home team gained greater conviction when Wertz slammed a two-run triple in the first inning. One could never have imagined that the Tribe would score only seven more runs the rest of the series.

That would certainly not be Wertz's most famous at-bat in the game. It can only be speculated whether the Indians would have avoided their funk had the arguably greatest catch in baseball history not robbed him in the eighth inning of the opener. With two on base and the score tied at 2–2, Wertz clobbered a pitch to dead center, into the vast expanses of the Polo Grounds. Giants center fielder and perhaps the finest player of all time Willie Mays tracked the ball with some form of inner radar and caught the 460-foot drive with his back turned to home plate. He then turned and fired the ball back in to catch Doby off second base for a double play that saved the game for his team.

The relative greatness of the snag has been argued over the decades. Some—including Mays himself—have claimed that he made better catches. Among those who considered it historically overblown was Bob Feller. Moreover, he believed Mays should have made the play in Hollywood rather than New York. "Yeah, we'd have scored some runs, but any center fielder—any decent center fielder—could have caught the ball," Feller said.

> *Willie put the act on pretty good. He could have caught the ball easy. And did, really. But Willie always did. He always wore his hat a little bit too big or too small so it would fall off. Ball hit right at him, he'd run over here and come back and dive for it. The ball was not all that tough. It hit into a little wind. It brought the ball straight down, like a popup over the infield. Over the catcher. And we knew he was going to catch the ball. Willie whirls around, throws the ball, his hat falls off. Greatest act I think since P. T. Barnum.*[2]

Doby certainly didn't know Mays was going to catch the ball or he would not have gotten caught off base for a double play that killed all Cleveland momentum for the series. And sensational or exaggerated in its difficulty, the snag allowed a little-known pinch-hitter named Dusty Rhodes to play the role of hero. Rhodes bashed a walk-off three-run homer off Lemon in the 10th to defeat the Indians. Little could anyone have imagined that it would be the first victory of four straight.

It has been offered that every team in every season goes through a slump. That is true only to varying degrees. But what is certain is that the Indians embarked on their worst slide of 1954 at the worst time. The bats that had pummeled American League pitching for 154 games simply went silent for four against the Giants. Lopez claimed with some validity that the series would have taken a different tone had the opener been played at Municipal Stadium, where the Wertz blast would have cleared the fence, as would the 420-foot triple he hit in the first inning, and likely would have resulted in a Cleveland victory, whereas the mere 270-foot Rhodes homer, which barely landed over the fence in the short Polo Grounds right-field porch, would have landed harmlessly in the glove of an Indians outfielder.

The Tribe continued to be tortured by Rhodes, the pinch-hitter extraordinaire who had batted .341 during the regular season. Rhodes slammed a game-tying single in the fifth inning and home run in the seventh of Game 2 as the Indians were held to one run—an Al Smith homer—in a 3–1 defeat. Lopez became testy after the loss when a media member asked him to identify its turning point to get him to admit it was when Doby could not catch the Rhodes single. The exchange was recorded by *Sports Illustrated* on October 11, just months after the legendary magazine was launched.

> *"What was the turning point today?" one reporter asked.*
>
> *"There wasn't any turning point," Lopez murmured.*
>
> *"There's got to be a turning point," the reporter insisted. "What was it?"*
>
> *"There wasn't any, I'm telling you," Lopez repeated, breaking out of a whisper.*
>
> *"Was the turning point when Doby couldn't catch that ball Rhodes hit?" the reporter persisted thickly.*
>
> *"Now goddam," Lopez shouted. "What are you trying to do. Ask your questions and answer them too? Goddam. What are you trying to do?"[3]*

What the Indians were trying to do was get healthy from the same home cooking that resulted in a mind-boggling 59–18 record at Municipal Stadium. Lopez believed a return to that familiar cavernous ballpark in front of sellout crowds would turn his team around. But the Giants had other ideas and battered Garcia for four runs in the first three innings. So shaken was the pitcher after Rhodes (who else?) singled in two in the third that he followed on the next play with a throwing error that cost him another run. The Indians never recovered, falling behind 6–0. Their lone highlight was a home run by Wertz. In fact, he was their lone highlight of the entire series. Wertz batted .500 in the four games (8-for-16). The rest of the team hit just .139 (18-for-121).

The outcome of the 1954 World Series had descended from desperate-but-hopeful to foregone conclusion in one day. The Indians played the early stages of Game 4 accordingly, falling behind 7–0 as Lemon was slammed for seven runs in four innings. Pinch-hitter Hank Majeski mashed a three-run homer in the fifth, but that fell under the category of way too little, way too late as his team went down meekly, 7–4. The most stunning sweep in baseball history was complete.

And what would be remembered most was what would become simply known as The Catch. Pirates general manager Joe E. Brown expressed his view a few weeks after the Indians had been doomed in Game 4 that the Mays effort forever changed the complexion of the series. But Brown believed it was the awareness of Mays after snagging the ball that turned the tide. "The catch itself was tremendous, but to me that wasn't the big thing and it's strange that not much attention has been given to it," Brown said. "It's what Willie did after catching the ball. He started to fall but as he did, he spun around and got rid of the ball. He made a strong throw off balance and while falling. Do you realize that if he had fallen down holding onto the ball, that runner might have scored all the way from second? That could have won the game for Cleveland and could have changed the whole series."[4]

Though one can only theorize on how the Mays catch and the series sweep changed the future of Indians baseball, some have offered that it altered the course of history, particularly regarding the competitive balance in the American League. Among those who claimed immediately following the four-game debacle that the Cleveland franchise would reel from it was Yankees general manager George Weiss. "I thought we would have a long, tough struggle to get back up there," he said. "Now, maybe not. I don't see how the Indians are going to recover from this."[5]

How well the Indians indeed recovered can be debated. They finished second to the Yankees in both 1955 and 1956, sunk into oblivion for the

Tribe slugger Vic Wertz smashed the drive that Willie Mays turned into an epic catch in Game 1 of the 1954 World Series.

COURTESY OF THE NATIONAL BASEBALL HALL OF FAME LIBRARY

next four decades, and have yet to win another world championship. But to believe that the events of the next seven decades were somehow influenced by one disaster of a World Series seems quite far-fetched. That it was simply five days of horror that had little or no bearing on the future would seem to be far more accurate an assessment. And every Indians fan would agree that losing four straight to the Giants was a picnic compared to the plight of the franchise in the decades that followed.

CHAPTER NINE

The Rise and Fall of Herb Score

CY SLAPNICKA KNEW A GREAT ARM WHEN HE SAW ONE. THE LEGENDARY Indians scout discovered Bob Feller in 1936. So when he cast an eye on a southpaw named Herb Score, that eye lit up. Fortunately for the franchise, Score was equally impressed with Slapnicka. Though he fielded higher offers, he signed with the Tribe for $60,000 in 1952.

Score boasted a Felleresque fastball. Like his predecessor, whose decline coincided with Score's rise, he overcame walks with strikeouts and weak contact. And when Score developed a fine curveball to go along with the heater, thanks to pitching coach Mel Harder, his penchant for stranding traffic on the bases became more pronounced.[1]

Score made minor leaguers look like little leaguers upon his arrival on the pro scene, which was delayed in 1953 by a broken collarbone. He tore up the American Association with Indianapolis the following season, winning the pitching triple crown by leading the league with 22 wins, an absurd 330 strikeouts in 251 innings, and 2.62 earned run average. That he earned Most Valuable Player honors was akin as a surprise to the sun rising in the east. Score allowed just 140 hits. And though he equaled that number in walks, he was ticketed in 1955 to join a formidable Cleveland staff that already featured Bob Lemon, Early Wynn, Mike Garcia, and an albeit fading Feller.

Score began blowing away everyone figuratively as he was blowing away batters. His fastball, at close to 100 miles an hour, inspired teammates and opponents to laud him as potentially one of the all-time greats—and he was just a 22-year-old rookie. Among those who were particularly impressed was young Indians slugger Rocky Colavito, who recalled his thoughts years later. "He was a great pitcher," Colavito said. "He had a chance at becoming as good a lefty as there ever was. He had that kind of stuff...[Hall of Famer] Sandy Koufax didn't win 20 [games] until he was 27. Herb did it at 23."[2]

The praise didn't stop with those wearing Indians uniforms. Red Sox slugger Ted Williams, who as arguably the greatest hitter of all time recognized great pitching when he saw it, claimed Score to boast the greatest fastball of any left-hander he ever faced. And Yankees second baseman Gil McDougald, whose one swing of the bat would forever alter the career of Herb Score and arguably the entire Indians franchise, stated succinctly that Score had Hall of Famer written all over him.[3]

The acclaim proved itself warranted. Score was no flamethrower who could not harness his talent. He set a major league rookie record for strikeouts in 1955 with 245 in his 227⅓ innings while posting a record of 16–10 and capturing the American League Rookie of the Year award. Major league hitters made him pay for his walks a bit more than their minor league brethren, so the conscientious Score worked to improve his control. He sliced his walk rate from 6.1 to 4.7 per nine innings in 1956, a key factor in raising his record to 20–9 and dropping his ERA to 2.53. Score proved overpowering typically and unhittable at his peak. Williams and the Red Sox found that out on May 1 when Score recorded all nine outs in the first three innings via the strikeout and ended the game with 16. He finished 1956 as the only pitcher in major league history to fan 200-plus in his first two seasons. And left-handed hitters might have felt tempted to forfeit their at-bats against Score. They batted a microscopic .123 against him that year. The Red Sox offered the then-hefty sum of $1 million for Score in March 1957 but Indians general manager Hank Greenberg turned it down, predicting that "Score may become the greatest pitcher in history."[4]

Nothing Score did in the first month of 1957 could have changed that optimism despite an alarming walk rate. He continued to pitch around his wildness, which included an 11-walk, complete-game performance in his first start. He had won four straight decisions heading into a home game against the vaunted Yankees on May 7. He retired Hank

Bauer on a groundout to open the first inning as Gil McDougald strode to the plate. The shortstop worked the count to 2–2, then smashed a line drive up the middle to which Score never had time to react. "I can remember seeing the ball coming right into my eye," Score explained. "Boy, it had got big awfully fast, and it was getting bigger. There was really nothing I could do about it."[5]

The liner slammed into the right eye, sending Score collapsing to the ground, and rolled to third base. *Sports Illustrated* painted the following picture of the scene: "The marvelous discipline of the game prevailed for another second or so—McDougald ran toward first and the Cleveland third baseman fielded the ball and threw it to first base for the curiously inconsequential out. Then players converged on the fallen pitcher. McDougald took one look and felt ill. Score, still conscious, was lying with his body in a defensive embryonic curve, bleeding frighteningly from the face. Amid an awful hush the loudspeakers called for doctors and a half dozen of them began hurrying across the grass."[6]

The tiniest of consolations, if one could be found, was that Score was spared a battle with Mickey Mantle, who kneeled on deck when tragedy struck. It was a moment the Hall of Fame slugger would never forget. "I remember hearing *pow-pow*, the bat hitting the ball, then the ball hitting Score," he said. "Just like that, almost with no time in between."[7]

The mound mechanics that contributed to his poor control also resulted in Score's inability to react. His powerful follow-through not only helped him fire the ball around 100 miles an hour but forced him to wear a pad on his right knee to cushion the blow when it hit his left elbow. That placed him out of position for fielding the ball and prevented him from seeing it clearly off the bat.

Score somehow kept his sense of humor and consciousness, asking those who surrounded him if boxer Gene Fullmer felt the same way when he was recently knocked out by Sugar Ray Robinson. And as he was being removed on a stretcher, Score told teammate Mike Garcia, "They can't say I didn't keep my eye on that one."[8]

McDougald was a sensitive soul. He stated, perhaps in a moment of weakness, that he would quit baseball if Score lost sight in his eye. It has been claimed that the incident negatively affected his career, though

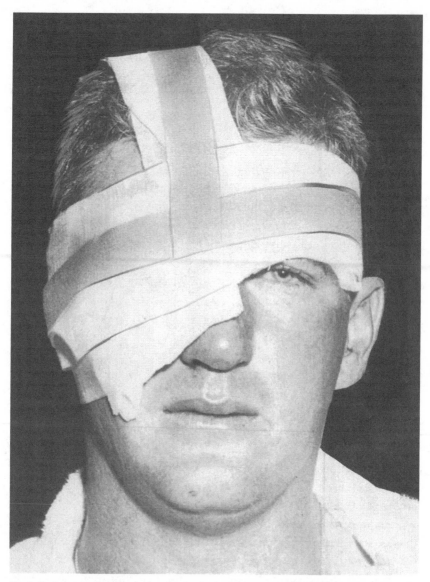

Herb Score was in sorry shape after the line drive that struck him in the eye.

Left-hander Herb Score was not the same pitcher in 1959 after the accident.
COURTESY OF THE CLEVELAND MEMORY PROJECT

such cannot be proved. McDougald, an American League Rookie of the Year winner in 1951, continued to thrive immediately after striking down Score and even finished fifth in the Most Valuable Player balloting that year. But his career took a decided downturn after that season in what should have been its peak. One can only speculate whether the lasting effect of any guilt he carried with him played a role in that decline.

What is certain is that McDougald felt heartsick in the aftermath. Unable to sleep that night, he accompanied Bauer and fellow Yankee Yogi Berra to the hospital to visit Score but was told that no visitors were allowed. Score's mother learned of McDougald's anguish and telephoned to assure him that he was blameless and urge him to stay active in baseball. Score himself messaged McDougald that what happened was simply part of the game. But McDougald continued to carry the burden along with him throughout his career. After Score returned to the sport and struggled, forcing a demotion to the minors, the devoutly Catholic infielder lamented that he had apparently not prayed hard enough. "I feel that I jeopardized a good living for him," McDougald said. "He had a lot of years ahead of him, good years. If there was anything I could do, I'd do it. But there's nothing. All I can do is pray."[9]

The sanguine Score embraced his usual glass-half-full attitude throughout his playing career and beyond. As he tried to emotionally and physically overcome the throbbing, torturous pain in his eye, which was covered for eight days, he grew thankful that he hadn't been killed rather than lament his misfortune. He felt lucky and gained a greater appreciation for his sight. And he moved up his wedding to high school sweetheart Nancy McNamara from October to July. After all, he certainly wasn't going to be playing baseball that summer.

Score refused throughout the rest of his life to blame the eye injury for his career downfall. He missed the remainder of the 1957 season but returned for the start of the following year. His inconsistency early in 1958 can be attributed to the long layoff. He was clobbered by lowly Kansas City on Opening Day but recovered to win in Detroit and shut out the White Sox on three hits while striking out 13. What he deemed to be the negative turning point of his career occurred in a loss to Washington on April 30. It was in the fourth inning that his elbow began to hurt, but he pitched through it, finally informing Indians manager Bobby Bragan in the ninth. The problem caused him to lose six weeks. Score insisted his claim that it was that injury that sent him spiraling to the depths was not made to spare the feelings of McDougald, but rather the truth. Either way, he was never the same. He pitched in only seven more games that year, starting once, giving up three earned runs and four walks while retiring only four Senators hitters in a mid-July defeat.

One can use hindsight and history to blame overwork. Score had thrown just 477 major league innings in 1955 and 1956 combined—pitchers in that era often averaged 250–300 innings per season—but his penchant for walks and strikeouts resulted in a huge pitch count. Yet the eye injury prevented him from pitching much from the time it occurred to the game in which he hurt his arm. One can only speculate that overwork played a role, but such a possibility seems a bit implausible. Pitchers often blow out their elbows or shoulders having thrown far fewer pitches than did Score early in his career. But it can be claimed that Bragan over-used him early in 1958, pitching him three times in the first five games, including once in relief.

Whatever the case, he was never the same. His elbow did not stop hurting until his mechanics were beyond repair. And he claimed that he had nobody to blame but himself for continuing to pitch. "I'd missed the whole year in '57 because of the eye injury and didn't want to miss any more time," he said. "So I kept throwing with a sore arm. I used to tell myself not to change my delivery to compensate for the soreness. But you do change your delivery; what once was natural because unnatural . . . I never had quite the same motion. I could still throw the good curve, but I couldn't throw the fastball like I used to anymore."[10]

The mechanical issues resulted in worse control than ever. Opposing batters continued to struggle to make consistently hard contact against Score. But they teed off on pitches Score could not spot on the corners. He allowed 28 home runs in 160⅔ innings in 1959, more than doubling his rate from his first two seasons, as his earned run average soared to 4.73. New manager Joe Gordon refused to bring him along slowly, allowing him to throw eight complete games in the first half of that year and using him in relief three times as well. He owned nine victories and a respectable 4.07 ERA at the All-Star break but lost all six decisions thereafter while compiling a terrible 6.31 ERA.

Score would never throw another pitch in an Indians uniform. General manager Frank "Trader" Lane dealt him to the White Sox for right-hander Barry Latman before the 1960 season in what was a steal for Cleveland despite the fact that the latter proved himself as little more than mediocre. Latman pitched for years for the Indians, managing an All-Star berth in 1961. Score lost the life on his fastball. His control descended from poor to awful. Even a trip to the minors to work on his mechanics failed. Score walked 113 in 144 innings over three seasons with Chicago and hung up his spikes in 1962.

He could have faded into the sunset. But Score reinvented himself and endeared himself to northeast Ohio as an Indians television and radio broadcaster. After three years in the TV booth, he replaced the legendary Jimmy Dudley on radio broadcasts, teaming with Bob Neal. The acerbic Neal had won a power play against Dudley—the two despised each other. But rather than trying to put the rookie on the radio in his place, Neal welcomed Score, who appreciated the help. "Bob Neal was the difference in my career," Score said. "If the professional broadcaster doesn't like the ex-athlete, he can make you look bad, and you have no chance. It happens a lot in this business. But Bob Neal never showed any resentment toward me."[11]

Score proved as genuine and unpretentious as a broadcaster as he was as an athlete. He refused to regale audiences with his exploits on the field, but rather quietly offered his expertise. Cleveland fans embraced his unpolished style and even forgetfulness that sometimes resulted in Score stating the wrong city in which the team was playing or mispronouncing

Herb Score (left) and Bob Neal teamed up to broadcast Indians games in the late 1960s.
COURTESY OF THE CLEVELAND MEMORY PROJECT

names. He worked as a play-by-play man to provide an objective viewpoint while rooting only with subtlety for the Indians. And his knowledge of the game was undeniable. "If I ran the Indians, Herb Score would be my general manager," stated fellow Tribe play-by-play broadcaster Joe Tait. "He is the smartest baseball man I've ever met."[12]

Score witnessed more than any other soul the longest stretch of ineptitude in baseball history. The Indians never sniffed contention from 1960 to 1993. Their rise and American League dominance over the following four seasons—the last of his career—was as much a gift for Score as it was for any fan. Unfortunately, he could not go out on cloud nine. His last broadcast was the most frustrating game in Indians history—the 3–2 loss in Game 7 of the 1997 World Series.

The rest of Score's life was filled with tragedy. He suffered hip, head, and pelvic injuries in a 1998 car accident, suffered a stroke four years later, battled a staph infection and pneumonia, then finally died in 2008. He was gone, but never forgotten for the class and dignity he brought to the Indians and northeast Ohio.

CHAPTER TEN

Launching the "Colavito Curse"

IT IS SILLY AND STUPID TO BLAME ONE DEAL FOR THE LONGEST PERIOD of franchise ineptitude in major league history. Or to superstitiously call it a curse. Long-term organizational success or failure in baseball is determined by financial health, talent evaluation, and a positive tip of the scales on all trades. But what can be justifiably claimed is that the 1960 swap of immensely popular slugger Rocky Colavito to Detroit for singles hitter Harvey Kuenn was among the worst in Indians history and sent shock waves through the clubhouse while turning off a generation of fans.

Colavito was the last remnant of the contending Indians teams of the mid-1950s. He had become a beloved figure in Cleveland, particularly among those in a significant Italian American community. He had blossomed into one of the premier power hitters in the sport, having bashed 83 home runs in the previous two seasons combined, including a league-leading 42 in 1959, when he led the team back into the pennant chase for what turned out to be the last time in 35 years and finished fourth in the Most Valuable Player voting. He was the team's lone superstar. He was generous with his time, often spending hours signing autographs.

Then came April 17. Little could Colavito or his teammates have imagined after he grounded into a force play during an exhibition game that day in Memphis that it would be his final game with the Indians uniform until the team recklessly and desperately got him back at the end of his career by shipping future Hall of Fame pitcher Tommy John and eventual All-Star outfielder Tommie Agee to the White Sox.

The moment that would live in infamy occurred after Colavito slugged a home run in his first at-bat. Following the groundout that landed him on first base, he was approached by manager Joe Gordon. Colavito figured he was about to be replaced because he had twice hit the ball hard and his swing appeared in fine shape for the regular-season opener two days later. But Gordon had some stunning news. General manager Frank "Trader" Lane had lived up to his nickname once again. "I remember it so clearly," Colavito told the *Los Angeles Times* in 1988. "He said, 'Rocky, that's the last time you're going to bat in a Cleveland uniform. You've just been traded.' I was in such shock. He said, 'Good luck' and all I could say was, 'Same to you.'"[1]

The immediate reaction in Cleveland was anger. Lane was hung in effigy. The fans could not believe he had traded their charismatic star. Colavito was the handsome dream boy of the bobby-soxers. He was the player that young boys dreamed of becoming as they played on the sand-lots and backyards of their neighborhoods. He performed with enthusiasm. The local media railed against the deal. The team was hit by a flood of season ticket cancellations that would play a role in a precipitous drop in attendance during Colavito's five-year absence. A *Plain Dealer* poll revealed that 90 percent of respondents were against the trade.[2]

Lane sought to bring logic into the conversation, but it fell flat. He claimed the team boasted plenty of power without Colavito and cited Kuenn's league-leading .353 batting average the previous year. Lane even stated wrongly that Kuenn could run, hit, and throw while all Colavito could do was slug long balls. Colavito, however, had established his arm as among the best in baseball. The trade was welcomed with open arms in Detroit, where a banner newspaper headline screamed out, "42 HOME RUNS FOR 135 SINGLES!" Despite his high average, Kuenn had not gained popularity in the Motor City.[3]

Colavito, who yearned to remain in Cleveland, felt Lane was motivated to trade him not for on-field considerations, but rather for one of the most poisonous emotions known to humankind—jealousy. The slugger's immense popularity, he believed, had stolen the spotlight away from

Fans express their displeasure in downtown Cleveland over the 1960 Rocky Colavito trade.

Lane, who was in the process of wrecking the team with irrational deals that sent future stars Roger Maris and Norm Cash packing. "It was ego. Pure ego, that's why he traded me," Colavito said.[4]

Adding delicious theater to the growing drama was the fact that the Tigers were scheduled to play in Cleveland to open the regular season. Nearly 53,000 fans cheered Colavito like he was still wearing an Indians uniform every time he stepped to the plate. He received a thunderous ovation before his first at-bat, which resulted in a strikeout. Colavito fanned four times in a hitless performance that also included a double play. He also misplayed a ball in the outfield, but his new team emerged with an extra-inning victory as Kuenn managed two hits in seven tries. Colavito, who admitted pronounced nervousness, later claimed it to be the worst game of his life. He made up for it the next day with a three-run homer that forged a tie as Detroit won again.[5]

Though the immediate results were far less decisive, the trade proved an unmitigated disaster for the Indians. Lane hoped to swap Colavito's ability to drive in runs for Kuenn's penchant for getting on base and scoring them. But the latter lost 45 points on his 1959 average and finished the season batting .308. He scored what was then a career-low 65 runs (he had tallied 99 in 1959) and drove in just 54. Though Colavito earned the wrath of Detroit fans with a comparatively unproductive season, he still slammed 35 home runs and drove in 87. Before the 1961 season, Trader Lane did it again by sending Kuenn to San Francisco for washed-up left-hander Johnny Antonelli and, strangely, power hitter Willie Kirkland, who could not hold a candle to Colavito. Colavito regained his greatness in helping the Tigers win 101 games that year, posting career highs with 45 home runs and 140 RBI, numbers that would have warranted MVP consideration had it not come in the same campaign in which Roger Maris and Mickey Mantle staged their epic battle for single-season home run supremacy.

The disillusionment of the Cleveland fandom grew increasingly evident in attendance numbers. The Indians attracted nearly 1.5 million fans in 1959, their largest figure in eight years. But after the trade of Colavito, it dropped precipitously. The team drew about 950,000 in 1960, 725,000 in 1961, 716,000 in 1962 despite remaining in strong contention through mid-July, 562,000 in 1963, and 653,000 in 1964. They ranked near the bottom of the American League in attendance in each of those seasons. But when Colavito returned in 1965 to lead the AL with 108 runs batted in, attendance soared to 934,000 and the Indians won 87 games, not so coincidentally their largest victory total since Colavito's last year in Cleveland.

As devastating as trading Colavito had been to the franchise, the cost of reacquiring him in 1965 proved more damaging. John went on to win 286 games after leaving Cleveland while Agee earned American League Rookie of the Year honors with Chicago in 1966, won two Gold Gloves, and helped the Miracle Mets of 1969 snag a World Series title.

Colavito was out of baseball by then. His second tour of duty with the Indians certainly proved to be more of a roller coaster ride than the first. Cleveland general manager Gabe Paul had finally succeeded in his desperate attempt to reacquire Colavito after what he claimed to be more than 100 offers to Detroit. He succeeded only after Colavito spent 1964 with the Kansas City Athletics and required a three-team trade. Colavito was thrilled. "I'm glad to be going home and I do mean home," he said. "Every year when I went into Cleveland with the Tigers or Athletics, I would say to myself, 'Wouldn't it be nice to be playing here again?'"[6]

The return of Colavito inspired 44,000 fans to stream into Municipal Stadium for the home opener. It was the largest Opening Day crowd in the majors that year and they were rewarded when their hero belted a two-run homer to key a victory. Colavito, fellow outfielder Leon "Daddy Wags" Wagner, and first baseman Fred "Wingy" Whitfield formed a slugging triumvirate that transformed the Indians into one of the top run-scoring teams in the American League while emerging power arms such as Sam McDowell, Sonny Siebert, and Luis Tiant spearheaded its most promising starting rotation.

Neither Colavito nor the promise of contention worked out. While John and Agee were gaining stardom, a shoulder ailment contributed to Colavito's early and rapid decline. He launched 30 home runs in 1966, but his batting average dipped to a career-low .238. Late-season struggles prompted new manager George Strickland to bench the prideful veteran. "I don't like it and I don't mind saying so," Colavito complained. "What really burns me is that I played all year with a sore shoulder and always tried to do my best. Now, with 12 games left, he is going to rest me."[7]

Colavito held out before the 1967 season. Paul asked him to take a major league maximum 25 percent pay cut. The two compromised, but Colavito did accept a lower salary. He stayed classy despite his disappointment, expressing hope of a bounce-back year that would recoup lost earnings. But it was not destined to happen under Joe Adcock, an experienced manager in what had become a revolving door at that position in Cleveland. Adcock moved Colavito from right field to left and platooned him with Wagner. Both players balked and struggled. The issue came to a head in a game at Fenway Park against Boston in which Colavito was lifted for a pinch-hitter with the bases loaded. A heated exchange between he and Adcock became public and led the *Cleveland Press* to take Adcock's side, criticizing Colavito for placing himself ahead of team interests and citing his holdout as evidence.[8]

Colavito was traded to the White Sox that July for nondescript outfielder Jim King, who managed just 21 at-bats for the Indians that year in concluding his career. Colavito gained some solace by socking a two-run homer off Tiant two days after the deal, but he too was done. He batted a meager .221 for Chicago the rest of that season and .211 for the Yankees and Dodgers in 1968 before retiring. He later served as an Indians batting coach and television analyst.

Before leaving Cleveland, he had been the leading vote-getter in a "Favorite Indian Contest" run by the *Plain Dealer*. And more than a half century later, he remains one of the favorite Indians of all time, not only for his baseball talents and production, but for his love for Cleveland and its fans.

CHAPTER ELEVEN

The Sad Saga of Sudden Sam

IT WAS ONCE BELIEVED BY OUTSIDERS THAT SAM McDOWELL WAS merely enigmatic. Frustrating. Baffling. A southpaw whose idiosyncrasies prevented him from maximizing his outrageous talent.

But his teammates knew. They understood that the man known as Sudden Sam was an alcoholic. If only the McDowell of 1968 could have consulted with the McDowell of 1998 who was helping major league players overcome substance abuse. Then perhaps he would have realized his potential. Because Sam McDowell had the stuff to be the Sandy Koufax of the American League.

Instead, he was a tease. He flirted with greatness, but never achieved it. The Indians and their fans waited for McDowell to turn all those strikeouts into victories. But then it would happen. He would throw a changeup to a terrible hitter such as Ray Oyler or Tom Matchick, despite the knowledge that he could pump his fastball right by them, and allow a game-tying single. Or he would lose his concentration and walk three straight batters to blow a two-run lead.

"I try to break things down to their simplest element," McDowell told *Sports Illustrated* in 1970, "and sometimes I guess I do it to an extreme. For instance, a game to me is just a series of individual challenges—me against Reggie Jackson or me against Don Mincher. If I find I can get a guy out with a fastball, it takes all the challenge away, so next time I throw him all curveballs. If I don't have a challenge I create one. It makes the game more interesting."[1]

McDowell appeared destined for the Hall of Fame at age 22 when he finished with a 17–11 record and league-leading 2.18 earned run average in 1965. But rather than continuing to blossom, he followed with marks of 9–8, 13–15, 18–14, 20–12, and 13–17. Even when he finally won 20, he was lambasted for performing under his potential. He feuded with Indians radio announcer Bob Neal, who publicly claimed McDowell had a million-dollar arm and 10-cent head. Granted, McDowell received little run support from the typically meager Cleveland offense. But neither did Robin Roberts with the 1950s Phillies and he led the National League in wins four straight years. Steve Carlton won 27 games for a 58-win Philadelphia team in 1972. Did McDowell simply not care enough about winning?

Nobody knew exactly. His motivations could never be deciphered through conversations with the media. He took a perverse pride in causing confusion, offering that reporters wrote what they wanted anyway, so he said whatever he wanted at the time. He stated at various points in interviews that strikeouts meant nothing to him and that his biggest thrill was his 1,500th career strikeout. He claimed that he never lost his temper and that he once became so angry at an umpire that he threw the ball into the upper deck in Baltimore. He said that records meant nothing to him and that he signed with the Indians to break all of Feller's records. He asserted that he worried too much about pitching and that he took his craft too lightly. He declared that he could never throw at a batter and that he would fire a fastball at his own mother if she tried to own the inside corner. And, in the ultimate contradiction, he contended that baseball meant everything to him and that baseball meant nothing to him.[2]

Opposing batters certainly appreciated the enigma that was Sudden Sam. It resulted in easier at-bats. McDowell boasted a deadly repertoire, but something was lost in the translation. And pitching for a weak-hitting Indians team during the lowest-scoring era in baseball history, one silly pitch, one short lapse of concentration, and a victory could be turned into a defeat. That happened all too often for McDowell. Among those who were all too happy to accept the gifts he often provided hitters was slugger Reggie Jackson.

Sudden Sam McDowell seen here in 1970 as he nears the end of his Indians career.

"Now don't get me wrong," Jackson said.

I like Sudden and I think he's got the greatest fastball, curveball, slider and changeup I ever saw. I call him "Instant Heat." But still, I don't mind facing him—and that's not because I hit him so easy, either. Because I don't. It's just that Sudden simplifies things out there. He makes it like it used to be when we were kids. You know he's gonna challenge you, his strength against yours, and either you beat him or he beats you. And if you beat him with a home run or something, hell, it don't bother him that much.[3]

It sure bothered and frustrated Indians fans. But as the 1960s moved along, those close to him such as teammates and coaches became aware that his failure to maximize his vast talents and his damaging personality traits were increasingly the result of his worsening alcoholism. McDowell later admitted being the biggest lush in the major leagues. During one spring training in Tucson, Arizona, he was arrested for drunk driving. The police offered to release him if Indians public relations director Ed Uhas picked him up. When Uhas arrived, he saw a staggering McDowell clinging to his cell. "Oh, no. Don't tell me they got you too, Eddie," McDowell exclaimed.[4]

Perhaps the team's eagerness to turn McDowell's big arm into a big success contributed to his downfall. Scouts had drooled over the lanky, 6-foot-5 southpaw during his prep days at Central Catholic in Pittsburgh. So talented was the four-sport standout that he often threw batting practice to the Pirates at Forbes Field near his home. He finished his senior season with an 8-0 record and a ridiculous 152 strikeouts in just 63 innings. The Indians offered him a then-hefty $75,000 bonus in outbidding 14 other teams. But his parents were wary about their son immediately jumping too many levels of competition, so they insisted he start in the low minors. The Indians obliged, sending him to Class D Lakeland, but not until his reputation as a young phenom landed him a spot on game show *To Tell the Truth*, where actor Tom Poston guessed his identity as a baseball player.

McDowell appeared destined to place his name among a long line of brilliant Indians hurlers, including those who headlined some of the greatest staffs in history during the 1940s and 1950s. He harnessed his control well enough in the minors to rapidly rise through the organization and make his major league debut in 1961. It was that spring in Tucson that *Plain Dealer* beat writer Bob Dolgan hung the "Sudden Sam" moniker on him as players described McDowell's fastball as arriving at the plate "all of a sudden." But some believe in hindsight that the Indians moved him along too quickly. He was promoted to Triple-A Salt Lake City that year and led the league in both strikeouts and walks. And six days before his 19th birthday, he was shutting out the Minnesota Twins into the seventh inning before a sore back prompted his removal. Sudden Sam would eventually reach superstardom. But he would never reach his potential.

Still painfully young and a bit confused by all the advice he was receiving from pitching coaches and managers, McDowell bounced from the majors to the minors over the next few years. He finally found a groove at Triple-A Portland in 1964, winning all eight decisions and boasting a tremendous 1.18 earned run average while walking just 24 in 102 innings. He hurled three consecutive shutouts, including a no-hitter in which he fanned 15. McDowell would soon be promoted to stay. He later explained his mound metamorphosis. "During those first four years, I listened to everybody and anybody who had a theory on pitching and I tried to do everything they told me," said McDowell, who credited Portland manager Johnny Lipon for making suggestions rather than demands. "I made up my mind to stop listening to everybody and figure out a few things on my own. I made up my mind I wasn't going to worry about my wildness, that I would throw where I wanted. By the middle of the [1964] season I could do it most of the time, at least with my fastball."[5]

McDowell appeared to have blossomed through 1965, but arm problems, lack of run support, and his own demons prevented a potential Hall of Famer from compiling any better than a 141–134 career record. Some complained that his many outside interests took his focus away from pitching. He collected and built guns, constructed model boats inside bottles, trained German shepherds, shot billiards, and painted still life. He also owned a pizza parlor and pool hall. The load of hobby-related stuff he carried on the road forced him to room alone. Such hobbies would not have been frowned upon, but some believed that he treated them with the same level of importance as he did his performance on the mound.[6]

Then there was what amounted to pitching suicide, the strange decisions on what pitches to throw to what batters. Second baseman Vern Fuller remembered one such occasion against Detroit. "Sam had something like 15 strikeouts after six innings," Fuller said.

> *I recall saying to [shortstop Larry Brown] that they had no chance against Sam. Larry said, "He won't strike another guy out." I don't know if he did strike out anyone else or not, but the point is that he started throwing his off-speed stuff, trying to trick [weak-hitting] Dick Tracewski. In this game we lost it when Sam threw a change-up to Ray Oyler. Think about that—Ray "Cotton Pickin" Oyler. He may have been the only guy who was a worse hitter than Tracewski. Ray Oyler couldn't hit Sam if Sam ran the ball across home plate, but Sam had to throw him slow stuff.[7]*

And, of course, there was the boozing. McDowell was no drinker before reaching the major leagues, but he certainly made up for lost time as he tried to assimilate with his teammates. Drunkenness among players was not uncommon—Mantle was a prime example—and Major League Baseball had yet to become enlightened enough to create outlets for therapy. The seeds of McDowell's losing battle with the disease could be traced to one evening after he had performed well against the White Sox. Fellow pitchers Gary Bell and Barry Latman took him out to celebrate the occasion.

"I respected them because they were established pitchers, and I appreciated the fact that they were paying attention to me," McDowell recalled. "Whatever Gary Bell ordered, I ordered. He ordered a drink, so did I. He ordered another drink, so I did. But when they stopped eating and drinking and went back to the hotel, I just stayed there and drank

Sam McDowell (second from right) congratulates Vern Fuller after a rare home run in 1969.

COURTESY OF THE CLEVELAND MEMORY PROJECT

some more. It was the first time I had been drinking and I didn't want to stop."[8]

His worsening alcoholism alarmed wife Carol and Indians general manager Gabe Paul, who sent McDowell to a psychiatrist whom the pitcher blew off after just one session. The disease had certainly taken hold of McDowell by 1971 when he was fined for his rowdy behavior on the team bus in Los Angeles and forced the team to ban alcohol on flights. McDowell finished just 13–17 that year with 153 walks in 214⅔ innings. His strikeout total plummeted from 304 in 1968 to just 192. And when he demanded a trade following that season, the Indians were eager to comply. They dealt him to San Francisco for proven veteran right-hander (and admitted spitballer) Gaylord Perry and surprisingly effective shortstop Frank Duffy in one of the most lopsided deals in team history. Perry won the Cy Young Award for the Indians in 1972 and tied an American League record with 15 consecutive wins in 1974 while McDowell continued to flounder with the Giants and eventually drink himself out of baseball.

McDowell hit bottom in 1980, five years after he retired from the sport. He recalled a frigid morning in Pittsburgh in 1980 in which he finally admitted to himself that he needed help. With the urging of his parents and brothers, he entered a rehabilitation center and cleaned himself up. "There was a horrendous inner pain, far more devastating than any physical pain," he said. "There was the feeling of always being alone, of always being on the outside, of something being wrong and you can never find out what. I can't say I chose to sober up or chose to get help. I quite frankly didn't think there was any hope. I didn't feel there was any way of helping me. I honestly thought I was going insane."[9]

It was too late to revive his career. McDowell would forever be known as one of the ultimate underachievers in Indians history. But he stopped drinking, began studying counseling, earned a degree in sports psychology and addictions, and started helping athletes in various sports avoid the same pitfalls that had swallowed him up. His impact on the generations of athletes to come proved far more important than any baseball game.

Chapter Twelve

The Tragic Tale of Tony Horton

IT WAS JUNE 24, 1970. THE INDIANS WERE LEADING THE HOST YANKEES, 7–2, in the ninth inning when 25-year-old Tony Horton stepped to the plate. Veteran reliever Steve Hamilton figured the time was ripe for his famous "Folly Floater," otherwise known as an eephus pitch. He lofted the ball about 25 feet skyward and it descended toward the plate. Horton took an uppercut hack and fouled it off. The fans roared with anticipation as Hamilton launched another one. Horton popped it up foul again, but this time it landed softly in the mitt of catcher Thurman Munson. The embarrassed slugger tossed his bat away, threw up his hands, walked toward the dugout, dropped to his hands and knees, and crawled in. Yankees announcer Phil Rizzuto shouted out his trademark "Holy cow!" and praised Horton for putting on a great show.[1]

One funny moment in one ballgame in one season, perhaps. But hindsight indicates a different story. And that is that the "performance" put on by Horton was just one manifestation of an emotional illness that would soon send him spiraling out of control and take one of the most promising hitters in Indians history with it. Horton, after all, was not one to joke around. Those who played alongside the tightly wound first baseman never even saw him smile.

Horton arrived in the big leagues with Boston in 1964, a year after immortal teammate Ted Williams, who was about to embark on his final season, praised him as a "natural" whose swing should not be tampered with. Horton, however, was forced to cool his heels, playing sparingly behind emerging Sox slugger George "Boomer" Scott nearly a decade before the advent of the designated hitter. After Scott nearly won American League Rookie of the Year honors, the Red Sox traded Horton to the Indians for veteran pitcher Gary Bell. Indians manager Joe Adcock placed him in his lineup immediately. Horton started slowly, but soon began to display his vast potential, going 22-for-42 during one torrid stretch in late July and early August to raise his average to .306. At age 22, he was already the team's best hitter.

Horton could have had it all. He was talented and disarmingly handsome. He had even starred in basketball as well as baseball in high school. He boasted a smooth, level swing that resulted in line-drive home runs rather than majestic blasts. He arrived in Cleveland as the heir apparent to Rocky Colavito.

But Horton took little joy in his craft. His intensity bordered on distress. He appeared to be trying to turn his bat into sawdust with every

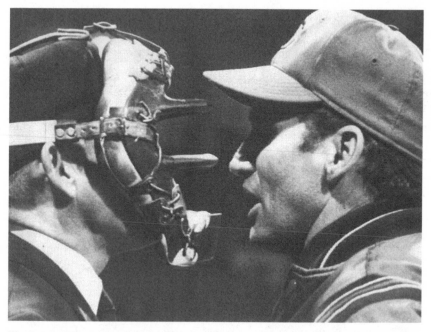

Manager Alvin Dark, seen here arguing with umpire Bill Valentine in 1968, saw the rise and fall of Tony Horton.
COURTESY OF THE CLEVELAND MEMORY PROJECT

Tony Horton chases a popup in vain in front of the typically empty seats at Municipal Stadium.
COURTESY OF THE CLEVELAND MEMORY PROJECT

trip to the plate. While others might let slumps and the accompanying boos roll off their backs, they tore Horton up inside. And he was a loner off the field, which prevented potential friends from helping. Rather than enjoying the fruits of his stardom, he toiled tirelessly on maximizing his talent. "Tony and I were roommates, and he is a good person," said pitcher Mike Paul. "He seldom drank. He had some dates but didn't really chase women. Being young and single, it would have been easy for him to be out on the town every night, but Tony had excellent personal habits. He was obsessed with success and thought he should hit 65 homers and drive in 200 runs every year. He took it as a personal failure every time he made an out."[2]

Horton confided only in his father—perhaps too much. "I was his first roommate with the Indians and I had to get away from him," said catcher Duke Sims. "He was just so intense, he couldn't ever relax. The fans in Cleveland, all 5,000 of them in those days, really got to him, too. Most of all, though, his father had an extreme influence on him. He had to talk to him every day."[3]

Some have speculated how that influence affected the inability of Horton to find contentment. Indians teammate Rich Rollins recalled how little happiness Horton found in playing the sport. "If I have one memory of Horton, it is that he never smiled, even after hitting a home run," Rollins said. "I was the guy who usually threw batting practice to Tony. . . . This wasn't a 15- or 20-minute thing, I mean, it went on at least an hour every time. I had heard about guys taking batting practice until their hands bled, but I never saw it until Tony."[4]

Those close to Horton believed the trade to Cleveland in 1967 heaped upon him a feeling of failure. Never mind that he would no longer be stuck behind Scott and would now be provided an opportunity to play every day. Rather than looking at the Indians as a team that wanted him, he saw himself as having been rejected by the Red Sox. But that did not prevent Horton from emerging as the team's premier power hitter. He impressed his teammates after blossoming in 1969 by batting .278 with 27 home runs and a team-high 93 RBI. "Tony was a stud," said third baseman Graig Nettles. "He was as good a hitter as I ever saw. You figured he was going to have a long and very productive career. But then one day he just went crazy."[5]

Some might claim the Cleveland fans drove him crazy. Their disenchantment with Horton stemmed from a holdout before the 1970 season. Horton, who used his father as an agent and never joined the Major League Baseball Players Association (MLBPA), demanded a hefty salary increase after his breakout year, but the Indians refused to even discuss it. Manager Alvin Dark suggested that Ken "Hawk" Harrelson could replace Horton at first base. That motivated Horton to accept the original Indians offer of $46,000. Ironically, Harrelson broke his ankle sliding into third base the day Horton signed. Horton believed the Indians would have been forced to give him a raise had he waited one day longer to put ink to paper. What followed was unmerciful booing from Cleveland fans. The media had proved unrelenting, portraying Horton during the holdout as a greedy punk.[6]

Dark later expressed regret for how Horton was treated, but stated plainly that the woebegone organization, which consistently ranked near the bottom of the American League in attendance, simply couldn't afford to pay Horton what he wanted. "I just knew we didn't have the money," Dark said. "Then, after Tony did sign, the fans really got on him. From day one that season, he was booed more than the average guy. I had no idea they would be so constant in their upset with Tony. He gave everything he had and just couldn't understand why they were booing him. As many times as I was fired, I'd have to say there was nothing more painful for me in baseball as my experience with Tony Horton where a life was almost ruined."[7]

Horton gave signs of his breakdown. Nettles recalled one day in 1970 when a zombielike Horton walked into the clubhouse and began rambling incoherently. Dark remembered being tapped on the shoulder after a game by shortstop Larry Brown. The players had begun shuffling back into the clubhouse. Brown pointed to Horton, who remained in his position at first base unaware that the contest was over.

What became Horton's last day in baseball nearly descended into his last day on earth. It was August 28, 1970. The Indians were playing a home doubleheader against the California Angels. Ace Sam McDowell, who preferred to be left alone before a start, was approached by Dark and told that Horton needed to speak with him. Rather than a uniform, Horton was wearing only underwear, a T-shirt, and shower shoes. Horton asked McDowell what he thought of him as a person. McDowell answered that he never considered Horton a friend because he couldn't understand him. A tearful Horton replied that he appreciated McDowell being honest and remained with the pitcher throughout his pregame routine. But when McDowell reached the bullpen to warm up, Horton had already left Municipal Stadium.

Other Indians were also approached before that game by Horton, who had visited every locker to offer his view about whether that player was a "man" or not. He began blathering about his view of manhood. "He wanted to know what I thought about him as a person," Vern Fuller said. "I think he was going to every player he could find, asking that same question."[8]

Soon Horton was headed to his home at the Blue Grass Motel (since torn down) on the outskirts of Cleveland, which boasted a bar frequented by many Indians players. One of its security personnel found him sitting in his car around 5 a.m., bleeding profusely after having slit his wrists. Horton was rushed to the hospital and never played again. His teammates picked up his belongings a couple days later. The attempted suicide remained a secret to the media. Throughout the rest of that season and the next, it was reported that he was convalescing or making progress, but simply not ready to return to baseball. That day never came.

"From what I understand, the doctors told him he had to completely divorce himself from baseball," McDowell recalled. "Baseball was what drove him to his state. He was so high-strung, with such a drive to succeed, and when he wasn't succeeding it set him off. It affected him every time he saw a former teammate or had a connection with baseball." *Plain Dealer* sports reporter Russell Schneider spoke with Horton in 1973. Horton sounded fine until the subject of baseball was broached. His voice began quivering and he said, "Baseball is no longer a part of my life and that's the way I want it."[9]

Any attempt to lure Horton out of his shell have proven fruitless. One media member visited him in Pacific Palisades, an exclusive Los Angeles suburb. Horton, who had forged a fine career in the banking industry, emerged from his gold Lexus with silver hair and gray T-shirt, plaid shorts and Nike cap. Horton was told by his father that a reporter wished to speak with him. "I'm not interested," he replied nicely. "You mean a sports story? I'm definitely not interested."[10]

That Horton could still not talk about baseball decades later shows how deeply he had been traumatized during his career. The weak-hitting

Indians could have benefitted from an emotionally and mentally healthy Horton during those dry years. But most important is that his attempt on his life failed and that he overcame his deep-seated problems. His journey certainly puts sports into perspective.

CHAPTER THIRTEEN

The Night That Will Live in Infamy

THE INDIANS WERE DESPERATE. THEY WERE CASH-STRAPPED. THEY annually ranked near the bottom of the American League in attendance. Threats to move the franchise to such cities as Seattle, Tampa, or New Orleans seemed frighteningly real. Not until Nick Mileti purchased the team in 1972 did that fear dissipate a bit among Cleveland fans. The Indians finished in the bottom half of the league in attendance every year but one (1965) from 1960 to 1992. They placed last 10 times during that woeful, barren period. They visited the basement in 1967, 1971, and 1973.

So anxious were the 1970 Indians to lure fans to see their lousy team that they plucked top draft pick Steve Dunning right out of Stanford University to pitch a Sunday afternoon game against Milwaukee. More than 25,000 fans—nearly three times the average crowd—flocked to Municipal Stadium to watch the wunderkind on the mound and he didn't disappoint, pitching five solid innings to beat the Brewers, 9–2. The money-hungry Indians did Dunning no favors by rushing him to The Show without minor league seasoning. He finished his career with a 23–41 record and bloated 4.56 ERA despite enormous talent.

The ruin of Dunning proved to have a negative long-term effect. But it did not hold a candle historically to one fateful night in 1974 that was motivated by the financial hardship plaguing the franchise for years. Not that attracting patrons through cheap beer was a new idea. The team gained success with a combined Nickel Beer and Helmet Day during Independence Day weekend in 1971 after the Astros and Brewers had done the same. Perhaps times had changed by 1974 and fans had become

93

unrulier. But it is more likely that the infamous 10 Cent Beer Night riot of June 4, 1974, resulted from a confluence of events and unfortunate circumstances.

The seeds of disaster had been planted by a team employee who suggested such a promotion to executive vice president Ted Bonda. Bonda agreed to give it a shot with beer.

The Rangers played a role in the impending disaster. A game between the two teams at Arlington Stadium on May 29 had descended into turmoil. The Indians and Rangers brawled, throwing punches after a beanball war. Plastic beer cups were hurled from the stands at Cleveland players. Indians catcher Dave Duncan tried to climb into the stands as he shouted at Texas fans while teammates dragged him back into the dugout. The media played up the incident, whetting the appetite and anger of Cleveland fans seeking revenge for a return visit by the Rangers.[1]

A comparative throng of 25,134 showed up on June 4—the first weekday crowd over 8,000 that season. And they were ready to do more than drink. Some arrived with firecrackers in their pockets. A portent of mayhem to come could be heard by anonymous explosions throughout the park from the start of the game. Peaceful fans and players grew a sense of unease as the proceedings continued. The first sign of the evening spiraling out of control belonged in a strip club rather than a ballpark. A chubby woman sitting along the first-base line jumped the wall and bared her breasts for the fans to see. She then attempted to land a smooch on home plate umpire Nestor Chylak, who refused the offer.[2]

Matters got a bit more out of hand in the fourth inning as Rangers batter Tom Grieve jogged toward third base after his second home run of the night. A streaker who had obviously embraced the fad that had gripped America at the time ran naked onto the field and slid into second base (which must have been painful). An inning later, two fans leaped over the outfield wall and mooned the Texas outfielders. The players became increasingly alarmed as park security chased an increasing number of numbskulls off the field.

The fans stepped up their verbal abuse on the Rangers, each of whom received lusty boos as they approached home plate. The patrons added fuel to their fire in the fourth when Indians hitter Leron Lee nailed future Hall of Fame pitcher Ferguson Jenkins with a line drive to the stomach. They took joy in his physical pain. "Hit him again, harder!" they chanted.[3]

Rangers fiery manager Billy Martin was not one to douse flames. Rather than avoid provoking a dangerous situation, he raced onto the field to argue a close play at third base in the fifth inning. A cascade of boos from the stands was accompanied by the hurling of a huge number of empty plastic cups from which fans had guzzled limitless amounts of beer. Martin blew kisses into the stands as he retreated into the dugout, further egging on those getting drunker by the sip.

The inebriated goofballs just kept coming. One tossed a tennis ball into center field, then ran after it, hugging another trespasser along the way while trying to elude security. Soon beer, rocks, golf balls, batteries, and anything else a fan could pick up and throw began raining down from the stands. A plea from the public address announcer to refrain from such activity had the opposite effect. Grounds crewmen who scrambled to keep the field clean were used as moving targets in what was quickly becoming a lost cause. Another woman jumped from the stands and was urged by the fans to disrobe as well. She did not comply, but she did attack ushers that tried to corral her, prompting boos and screams claiming police brutality.[4]

Why the Indians did not bolster police presence for an event billed as 10 Cent Beer Night is anybody's guess. Why they allowed fans to line up behind outfield fences and refill their cups from a Stroh's company truck when demand overcame supply at the concession stands is also baffling. The result was a situation that descended from barely controllable to mayhem. One fan tossed lit firecrackers into the Texas bullpen, which prompted Chylak to evacuate both bullpens as relievers were forced to warm up on the mound. A jug of wine nearly landed on the head of Rangers first baseman Mike Hargrove, who ironically would go on to play with and manage the Indians. Fans casually stripped and streaked across the field, leaving their clothes on a heap in the outfield. Sober patrons, some fearing for their safety, began leaving in droves with their families. The cops simply could not keep up.

"The policemen are overweight, elderly guys who've got belts on with billy clubs and walkie-talkies and guns," recalled Indians director of sales and marketing Carl Fazio. "They have to put their hands on their side to hold all this stuff so they can run after these kids, and here are these 19-year-old kids, cutting on a dime and these older guys with all this equipment trying to keep up with them and the crowd started laughing at the policemen. That was a bad sign right there."[5]

All hell broke loose in the ninth, after the Indians rallied to tie the game at 5–5 and placed the winning run on second base. A sloshed fan leaped onto the field and flipped the cap off the head of Rangers outfielder Jeff Burroughs. Burroughs tripped and fell as he turned toward the inebriate, prompting his bat-wielding teammates to charge to the scene. A mob of about 200 fans brandishing whatever makeshift weapons they could find, including knives, chains, and clubs, stormed the field to attack the Rangers. Indians manager Ken Aspromonte ordered his players to

Texas Rangers manager Billy Martin (left) and players Jeff Burroughs and Joe Lovitto grab bats to defend themselves.
COURTESY OF THE CLEVELAND MEMORY PROJECT

save their fellow ballplayers. Cleveland players joined the fray, bats in hand. What followed can only be described as a riot. The umpires forfeited the game to Texas and the players eventually escaped to the safety of their clubhouses, but not before several players had been battered and bloodied. Among those beaten was local sportswriter Dan Coughlin, who was twice socked in the face while interviewing fans.

Indians play-by-play radio broadcaster Joe Tait described the scene. "Tom Hilgendorf has been hit in the head. Hilgy is in definite pain," he said. "He's bent over, holding his head . . . Aw, this is an absolute tragedy . . . I've been in the business for 20 years, and I have never seen anything as disgusting as this." Aspromonte blamed not just the fans, but society in general for the breakdown in law and order. Chylak was not nearly as

Bloodied Indians reliever Tom Hilgendorf is escorted off the field by a security guard.
COURTESY OF THE CLEVELAND MEMORY PROJECT

kind as he treated his bleeding head. "Fucking animals!" he decried. "You just can't pull back a pack of animals. When uncontrolled beasts are out there, you gotta do something. I saw two guys with knives, and I got hit with a chair."[6]

Umpire Joe Brinkman leads a bleeding fan off the field.
COURTESY OF THE CLEVELAND MEMORY PROJECT

And when it was all over, there was plenty of blame to go around. Some of it was placed squarely on Martin and the media. When asked before the trip to Cleveland if he was worried about retribution from Cleveland supporters after the debacle in Texas, the combative manager stated that the Indians didn't have enough fans to worry about. That added fuel to the fire of acerbic, highly entertaining Cleveland radio sports talk show host Pete Franklin, who spent much of the lead-up to the game calling for revenge. "He was on the radio every night promoting vengeance against the Rangers for the brawl," remembered Coughlin.[7]

One can only speculate how the events of that fateful evening affected the Indians on the field, but they rebounded to embark on their strongest stretch of the decade and beyond. They won 21 of their next 30 games to ascend to the top of the American League East as Gaylord Perry tied an American League record with 15 consecutive victories. They remained within shouting distance of the lead despite a 71–70 record on September 11 before collapsing. Their flirtation with contention resulted in surpassing one million in attendance for the first time in 15 years. But despite that albeit limited success, 1974 in Indians history would forever be linked to the 10 Cent Beer Night fiasco—and for good reason.

What seemed like madness, however, was a desperate attempt to attract fans, as Fazio later explained. "If you put on the hindsight glasses and kind of dumb it down, you're missing the context in which we were operating," he said. "We were on a mission to save baseball in Cleveland. We were bound and determined to do everything we could—the team, special events, promotions, the whole ballpark experience. We did every-thing possible to make baseball successful in Cleveland."[8]

It would take two more decades and a new ballpark for that dream to become a reality.

CHAPTER FOURTEEN

Putting the Cherry on Top

THE INDIANS HISTORICALLY HAVE NOT TAKEN THE LEAD IN MUCH. Nearly every team that can trace its history back a century or longer has won more pennants and world championships. But the Cleveland organization has dominated in one category. And that is breaking color barriers.

The Tribe became the first American League team to sign an African American player when they debuted Larry Doby in 1947. And though it can be argued that had greater significance, the move that received far more attention was their hiring of Frank Robinson as the first black manager in the major leagues in 1975. That he was utilized as a player-manager resulted in greater pressure and attention. That made his heroics on April 8 even more remarkable.

Robinson had already established himself as a first-ballot Hall of Famer upon his arrival. The 19-year veteran won National League Rookie of the Year honors with Cincinnati in 1956 and remains the only player to win the Most Valuable Player award in both leagues. He even won the Triple Crown with Baltimore in 1966 and finished his career with 586 home runs. But Robinson's gifts extended far beyond the physical. His fiery nature, drive to win, and natural leadership abilities combined to inspire others to cite him as the ideal candidate as the first African American manager long before it happened.

The seeds were planted on September 12, 1974. That is when they signed Robinson as a player, though speculation about their intentions raged immediately. The Indians ostensibly snagged Robinson off waivers

Frank Robinson awaits his first at-bat as player-manager in 1975—and first home run.

WIKIMEDIA COMMONS, COURTESY OF PAUL TEPLEY

from the Angels as a potential booming bat for the stretch run. General manager Phil Seghi and Robinson denied any other motivation. But the expressed interest in Robinson as an offensive force failed to bear fruit—he batted just .200 with two home runs in 50 at-bats as the Indians fell apart. Some have speculated that the uncertainty over who would manage the team in 1975 contributed to the collapse. It certainly angered Gaylord Perry, whose dislike for Robinson (and vice versa) had been well-established during their days in the National League. Perry, a white Southerner, and Robinson, a tough, more militant, new-breed African American, did not see eye to eye. And in late September, Perry told the media of his plan to ask the Indians for "the same salary, plus a dollar more" than the $173,500 annual income earned by the two-time MVP.[1]

Bruised egos and career upheavals were transformed into anger and violence as the team waited out a rain delay on September 27. The firestorm began when Aspromonte asked Seghi point-blank if he would return as manager the following year. Seghi informed Aspromonte of his lame-duck status but requested he keep things quiet until after the season. A distraught Aspromonte returned to his office, only to be forced to respond to a ruckus in the clubhouse. Robinson had confronted Perry about the contract demand played out in the papers. The two might have struck blows had Aspromonte not separated them. The manager also decided to defy Seghi and announce that he would not be back in 1975. What was strongly suspected became official on October 3: The Indians had hired Frank Robinson as the first African American manager in baseball history.

The reaction was immediate and positive. Major League Baseball commissioner Bowie Kuhn provided the following message: It's about time. "Now that it has happened, I'm not going to get up and shout that this is something for baseball to be exceptionally proud of, because it is so long overdue." The same level of dismay over how team owners dragged their feet about hiring a black manager has been expressed given the hindsight of history. "What's really extraordinary is how long it took and, on a certain level that it should be significant for what should have been a routine progression after Jackie [Robinson broke the color barrier as a player]," stated baseball history expert and history professor at San

A feud with Frank Robinson ended the Cleveland career of Hall of Fame pitcher Gaylord Perry.

COURTESY OF THE NATIONAL BASEBALL HALL OF FAME LIBRARY

Francisco State University Jules Tygiel. "The major leagues weren't ready for that step."[2]

Neither, apparently, were some Indians players, though one can speculate that their beef with Robinson was purely based on managerial decisions.

The battles with Perry can best be described as the Clash of the Titans. Perry arrived in Cleveland as a savior, winning the Cy Young Award in 1972 and establishing himself as one of the premier pitchers in the American League, just as he had in the National League. His epic winning streak in 1974 not only allowed the Indians to soar into first place, but temporarily awoke a sleeping giant. Perry lured fans into creaky old Municipal Stadium. And Robinson was simply one of the greatest players of all time. They were two superstars with massive egos and clashing motivations who placed themselves on a collision course early in 1975.

Fortunately, not too early. Not on Opening Day. Not in one of the most historic events in Indians history—certainly the greatest from what has become known as the bad old days. The date was April 8, 1975. After Perry blanked the Yankees in the first inning, Robinson stepped to the plate as the second hitter in the lineup and mashed a Doc Medich pitch into the frigid air and over the left-field fence for a home run. The crowd of 56,715 roared its approval. Perry did the rest, going all the way for the victory as aging slugger Boog Powell, who was Robinson's teammate in Baltimore, homered and doubled to aid the cause. Robinson was ecstatic after his first managerial triumph. "Right now, I feel better than I have after anything I've ever done in the game." Strong stuff considering he'd helped the Orioles win the World Series in 1966 and 1970.[3]

The good vibrations didn't last. Upon his arrival in 1974, Robinson perceived the Indians to be a segregated bunch, both among the players and coaching staff, which included Larry Doby, the first black player in the American League. Perry openly complained before the regular season about the training regimen instituted by his new manager, including 15 sprints from foul pole to foul pole and backwards running. Perry, who was no Jack LaLanne, preferred to take his conditioning at his own speed. "I am nobody's slave," he told a reporter controversially and undiplomatically, adding, "The way this place is run is really chickenshit." The right-hander was merely scratching the surface of his subversives toward Robinson's rule.[4]

While the fiery Robinson tried to ignore Perry's antagonism, the pitcher kept tossing beanballs. He questioned Robinson's handling of the players. He slyly attracted the attention of teams with which he preferred to play, such as the Red Sox and Rangers, through quotes picked up by the media. It had become evident that the two could not coexist. The feud was bringing the entire team down. Perry—as well as brother Jim, who had also performed well for the Indians in 1974—were pitching poorly.

Robinson made history, but he also made enemies with a combative style and, eventually, a defensiveness to criticism. Race played a role in his reactions to events, such as an argument with umpire Bill Haller, during which he pointed to the color of his skin and asked, "Does this bother you?" Robinson was even suspended by the league for three games and fined for bumping umpire Jerry Neudecker. By the All-Star break in 1975 he had already been ejected from games three times. He accused umpires of prejudice against his team, a remark that could clearly be construed as believing they made calls against the Indians because he was black.[5]

Perry was traded to Texas on June 13 for serviceable starters Jim Bibby, Rick Waits, and Jackie Brown, giving the team badly needed rotation depth. The deal also brought a breath of fresh air to a team that had been rotting from the inside. So did the emergence of standouts such as brash, side-arming right-hander Dennis Eckersley and center fielder Rick Manning. Their youth and willingness to follow Robinson's lead infused the team with confidence and enthusiasm. The Indians bottomed out at 24–39, then won 13 of 17. Another losing stretch was followed by an 18–5 run. Robinson refused to allow his team to quit or be overwhelmed by stronger and more experienced competition. The Indians finished the season at 79–80, their best record since 1968.

The new wave of Indians indeed appreciated Robinson far more than some of the veterans. Among them was Eckersley, who did not mind the manager's tough style. "Frank Robinson had a lot to do with my development," said the future Hall of Famer. "There were games where I'd go crazy on the mound, screaming at everyone. It just poured out of me. Frank would scream, 'Grow up' right back at me. A couple of times he dumped on me in front of all the other players. He made me small, but that was okay. I needed it at that time in my career. Frank would take Rick and me out drinking a couple of times, and we talked the game. He took great care of us. He was the best manager Rick and I could have had. We loved the guy, and we loved being with the Indians back then."[6]

In the end, however, Robinson became just another Cleveland manager who wore out his welcome. His Indians hung around .500 throughout 1976, never falling more than six games under or ascending more than six games over. The team simply did not boast the talent to contend but managed its best record in eight years. Robinson lost the team in 1977 and it was incidents involving black players that doomed him. African American infielder Larvell Blanks went berserk in the clubhouse, tossing equipment and clothing from his locker and kicking a stool that smashed into a full pot of coffee. He then refused to speak with Robinson in the manager's office.

But it was black Latino Rico Carty, the team's best hitter, who clashed most vehemently with Robinson. The seeds of discontent were planted in 1976 when Robinson bawled him out for getting ejected for swearing at an umpire over a strike call. Standing just three feet away from Robinson during a Wahoo Club luncheon three weeks into the 1977 season, Carty accused his manager of lacking leadership. Their relationship became irreparable. Carty grew angrier on June 1 when Robinson expressed no interest in his pulled hamstring. Robinson claimed five days later that Carty loudly second-guessed his moves in the dugout.[7]

The manager was losing control of his team. He even lost the support of legendary play-by-play broadcaster Joe Tait, who strongly criticized Robinson on a sports talk show and in an interview with the *Plain Dealer*. "I don't think Robinson has the mental or emotional capacity to manage well," Tait said. "It's tough for a superstar to communicate with guys of less talent. I just don't think Frank knows how to stir them up the way he stirred himself up when he played."[8]

The end was near. And it came on June 19, after the Indians had won two straight against Detroit to launch a nine-game winning streak. Seghi had wanted to fire Robinson after the 1976 season, but owner Ted Bonda gave him a bit more rope. Some believed that firing Robinson after he

Rick Manning, seen here sliding safely in third, gave Frank Robinson hope for the future.
COURTESY OF THE CLEVELAND MEMORY PROJECT

had guided the team to its best record since 1968 would have smacked of racism, but Bonda later denied such an allegation. "There wasn't any pressure," he said. "Actually, the black fans never materialized in the park, although I know they took pride in him. It certainly had no effect on the firing."[9]

Robinson believed the lack of support from Seghi and Bonda in 1977 enabled the players to defy him, though some might believe that was merely the paranoid thoughts of a doomed manager. "The thing that made it difficult was that the players knew I did not have the support at the top," he claimed. "If the players sense that a manager does not have front-office support, he's not going to have full control. And once he doesn't have full control over the players, the situation becomes very, very difficult on the field."[10]

Replacement Jeff Torborg fared worse. The 1977 Indians collapsed after peaking at 33–31, embarking on a 13–31 slide, recovering for a while, then ending the year 8–19 to finish the season at 71–90. Robinson

Rick Manning scores against Texas in 1981 as his disappointing Indians career neared its end.

went on to manage four other teams and win American League Manager of the Year honors in 1989 for turning around the woeful Orioles. And through rose-colored glasses and the magic of time, his stay in Cleveland will always be remembered for his Opening Day home run in 1975 that brought fans to their feet and put hope in their hearts.

In fact, a statue of Robinson was built outside Progressive Field and he spoke at an unveiling ceremony in 2017. "I never thought I'd be here for something like this," he said.[11]

Neither would have anyone else 40 years earlier.

CHAPTER FIFTEEN

Drowning in Free Agent Waters

IT WAS 1974. THANKS TO THE BRILLIANCE AND PERSEVERANCE OF Major League Baseball Players Association executive director Marvin Miller, the reserve clause had met its demise and the premier talent in the sport were gaining the right to auction themselves off to the highest bidder. The new era of free agency, one that would eventually result in $30-million-a-year contracts, had begun.

The Indians wanted in. They yearned to end more than a decade of mediocrity and terrible attendance by luring the top sluggers and hurlers to Municipal Stadium. There was just one problem: They barely had enough money to pay their own cheap players, let alone the Reggie Jacksons and Catfish Hunters of the world. But it was a chicken-and-egg thing. They believed they had to spend money to make money. So they offered Hunter $2 million.

The crafty right-hander was coming off a 25-win season in which he had won the American League Cy Young Award. Hunter had exceeded 20 victories in each of the previous five years. He had led baseball with 30 complete games in 1974. And he had played the entire campaign without a contract so he could earn his freedom. The big bucks offered by the Indians seemed justified. They even had Gaylord Perry call his North Carolina friend to lure him to Cleveland.

No dice. Hunter signed instead with the Yankees for $3.2 million over five years and proved unworthy of the length of the contract, managing two fine seasons before petering out.

The Indians remained undaunted. They perceived the need to add a co-ace to replace the departed Gaylord Perry and team with brash side-arming right-hander Dennis Eckersley, who was emerging as an all-star. So they targeted Orioles righty Wayne Garland.

Was Garland a logical choice? One could argue in either direction. He had blossomed in 1976 with a 20–7 record and 2.67 earned run average, having transformed his screwball into a lethal pitch. But he was far from established. He had managed just that one great season after having been previously stuck behind the mainstays of the deep and talented Baltimore staff. Indeed, Garland did not have much of a track record. He was also a control pitcher rather than a power one who could not overcome mistakes with velocity. But the Indians believed Garland was on the doorstep of greatness.

The 26-year-old explained in an interview 12 years later what happened next. He had been hoping for a million-dollar deal. His wildest dream was about to become reality when he received a call from agent Jerry Kapstein. "He said, 'Wayne, I didn't get you a million dollars,'" Garland recalled. "I said, 'Jerry, I'm sure you did the best you could.' He said, 'You got a 10-year contract for over $2 million.' I said, 'Jerry, I'm not worth it.' He said, 'Well, obviously someone thinks you are.'"[1]

And that was the Indians, who had offered $2.3 million spread over a length of time they believed they could handle financially, though they decided to pay now and consider the consequences later. Garland would have been a steal by the end of the deal had he continued to perform annually as he had in 1976. But after his first season, he spent more time on the disabled list than on the active roster and was out of baseball after 1981. He collected paychecks from the Cleveland organization for the next five years.

Moreover, though he tried to live up to his contract, he proved himself to be an unbearable person, scowling with his mouth closed and complaining with his mouth open. One might have assumed his unhappiness stemmed from his inability to pitch as well as he did in Baltimore, but Hall of Fame manager Earl Weaver reported that Garland was no different when he was racking up victories with the Orioles.

Wayne Garland was nearly washed up when shown here in 1979 spring training.
COURTESY OF THE CLEVELAND MEMORY PROJECT

"You know what his nickname was with us?" Weaver asked. "We called him Grumpy. The guy was a big grouch when he was winning 20 games for me in 1976. I had to run him to the mound four times in September so he'd win that 20th game, and he bitched about it the whole time." About what? "Everything . . . anything," Weaver added. "With Wayne, who knows? And I found it better not to listen. He's really not a bad guy, but he just acts so unhappy all the time."[2]

There was certainly something wrong if he was unhappy upon learning of the Indians' offer. After all, the average major league salary at the time was $50,000 and all-stars earned only double that. But free agency launched a new ballgame that will be played forever. If Garland ever cracked a smile, it was when he signed that deal. "I was flabbergasted," he said. "The last thing I expected was that kind of money. I never asked for that much. I never even dreamed I'd make that much. But what was I supposed to do, give it back? . . . For that kind of money, I'd have played in Siberia."[3]

Perhaps that was a Freudian slip, but Cleveland was certainly considered the Siberia of the major leagues at the time. But the organization believed one hand could wash the other. They figured Garland boasted the talent to transform the Indians from Siberia to the French Riviera. He was just 26 years old and owned a 20-win season. The Indians perceived the potential for a wonderful return on their investment. And with free agency certain to raise payrolls exponentially, giving Garland $230,000 seven or eight years from then did not feel foolhardy.

One might figure with the luck of that franchise in the 1970s that Garland hurt his arm at some point in the 1977 regular season. But no. He injured it *warming up for* his *first spring training game*. His arm felt stiff, but he yearned to pitch through it to begin justifying his contract and developed a sore arm. Rather than shutting himself down, he endured the pain and performed to the best of his ability. The result was a 13–19 record and decent 3.60 earned run average in his first season with the Indians before circling and heading down the drain.

Garland and the Indians performed horribly early in the year. He allowed 19 runs in his first 17⅓ innings for a 9.87 ERA and lost his first four decisions. After a stretch of inconsistency in which he pitched well only occasionally through mid-June, he owned a 2–7 record and 5.60 ERA. Fans booed Garland unmercifully, making a melancholy man even more miserable.

"What was rough," Garland said, "was when I'd be on the mound and guys in the stands would be using the most abusive language you can imagine, and my wife and three kids are there having to hear it."[4]

Garland could not be accused of sitting on the newfound wealth of his guaranteed contract. He hit his stride around midseason despite the discomfort in his arm, pitching 17 complete games the rest of the way, going nine in his last seven starts. He finished the year with 282⅓ innings pitched. He turned in 15 quality starts in his last 16 outings.

That would be his last hurrah. His arm would never again allow him to pitch better or more often. Garland opened the 1978 season in the rotation, but never made it through April. After posting a 7.07 ERA in his first five starts, he took the mound in Oakland and surrendered five runs by the second inning. Even his one-time pinpoint control was gone. He had walked 16 batters in 29⅔ innings. And his arm was killing him.

Garland could not isolate the moment in which the health of what was once a healthy right arm began deteriorating, but he had understood even in 1976 that nothing lasts forever. He just didn't know it would happen that quickly. "I wish I could pinpoint it," he told the *Los Angeles Times* in 1988. "Like the doctor told me, you only have so many pitches left in your arm."[5]

Noted surgeon Frank Jobe diagnosed a torn rotator cuff, which could have been prevented or at least treated before it reached an alarming stage had Garland pitched in the late 1980s and beyond. He might have been able to nurse his arm back to health had he shut himself down at the first sign of soreness and Indians manager Frank Robinson not left him on the mound to toss one complete game after another. But such caution grew far more prevalent after Garland was forced to retire following his release by the Indians in January 1982. He managed a record of 15–29 in his last four years with Cleveland, much of which was spent sidelined after the rotator cuff surgery in 1978 failed to yield the desired results. Desperate to resume his career, he worked with legendary knuckleballer Hoyt Wilhelm to learn that pitch, which is significantly less stressful on the arm, but he eventually stared at the writing on the wall. "I said, 'You've had your career. It's time to get out.'"[6]

Garland had not endeared himself to Cleveland fans, though they grew respectful of his perseverance. They had complained about his splurging for a $750,000 stone mansion in the wealthy suburb of Gates Mills that featured a tennis court, a swimming pool, and riding stables. Two accompanying homes served as maids' quarters. Fans perceived his $250,000 down payment and $450,000 mortgage as proof that he had become corrupted by his huge payday.

The Garland fiasco proved a fitting end to a horrific decade in Indians history, one marked by near financial ruin in which they tried to patch up one leak while water poured from another. They had traded their most promising players, ones that earned long-term greatness, such as Chris Chambliss, Graig Nettles, and Dennis Eckersley, to the Yankees and Red Sox, respectively, for players that provided one or two decent seasons. And when they tried to spend big money on a free agent, it bit them right in the butt. One might have believed they had hit rock bottom and their luck was about to change. But what became known as the Curse of Rocky Colavito would remain in overdrive for many years.

CHAPTER SIXTEEN

Super Joe Charboneau

THE TALES OF FEATS GREW WITH THE HANDS OF TIME. HE DRANK BEER through his nose. He cut out a tattoo with a razor. He played "The Incredible Hulk," a game in which others would break giant rocks against his chest with smaller ones until all had been smashed into dust. He stitched a cut with a fishing line. He opened cans with his eye socket. And he hit the hell out of the ball—at least for one season. Only the last claim was certainly true.

He was the legendary Super Joe Charboneau.

The Paul Bunyan figure captured the imagination of win-starved Cleveland baseball fans in 1980. No one player could transform the Indians of that era into a champion, but Charboneau certainly infused some energy into cavernous and usually empty Municipal Stadium. He came out of nowhere to emerge as the team's most popular player and its premier power hitter. So enamored did Indians followers become with Charboneau that local band Section 36 wrote a short ditty honoring him titled "Go Joe Charboneau" that reached No. 3 on the local charts. Some of the lyrics, interspersed with the radio play-by-play of a Charboneau home run, were as follows:

> *Who's the one to keep our hopes alive?*
>> *Go Joe Charboneau*
>> *Straight from the 7th to the pennant drive?*
>> *Go Joe Charboneau*

Raise your glass, let out a cheer
Go Joe Charboneau[1]

Charboneau proved to be the ultimate flash in the pan, but the idio-syncrasies that made him a legend were genuine, not produced once he reached the big time to gain publicity. His early life, in fact, was peppered with incidents that could have proven tragic had his talent not won over. He was a brawler who was booted out of elementary and middle school due to poor grades. His mother later spoke of his concentration issues that would have resulted in a specialized learning tack in the modern era. Charboneau, who spent time in Illinois, Michigan, California, and Oregon during his youth, displayed his skills on the diamond in high school, but his erratic behavior threatened to prevent him from maximizing his potential. He engaged in bare-knuckle battles with migrant workers to make money and specialized in taking dangerous dares.

Charboneau could thank high school teammate Steve Bartkowski for getting noticed. He caught the attention of Phillies scout Eddie Bockman, who had been dispatched to watch the future Atlanta Falcons star quarterback. Bockman continued to follow Charboneau, who had enrolled at West Valley College, where he batted .373 while leading the conference with 12 home runs. He was eventually picked by the Phillies in the second round of the 1976 draft. After a strong start to his professional career, he was benched at Class A Peninsula and quit baseball to take a job as a store clerk in Santa Clara. Bockman soon convinced him to give the sport another shot. He immediately flourished, winning the Carolina League batting championship and driving in 116 runs. His antics, however, frightened off the Phillies, who traded him to the Indians. Charboneau batted .352 at Double-A Chattanooga in 1979 and earned a spot with the big club in spring training the following year.

A bad break for the Indians and slugger Andre Thornton proved to be a great break for Charboneau. A knee injury ended Thornton's season before it began, opening the door for Charboneau. His legend grew when he smashed a home run on Opening Day in Anaheim and another in the home opener, during which he also singled and doubled. And in his first trip to Yankee Stadium, where legends are made, he rocketed a blast into

Super Joe Charboneau proved to be the ultimate one-hit wonder for the Indians in 1980.

COURTESY OF THE NATIONAL BASEBALL HALL OF FAME LIBRARY

the third deck of the left-field grandstands, where only Jimmie Foxx and Frank Howard had slugged one before.

"I remember it like it was yesterday," Charboneau later recalled. "As I was going around second base, I looked up to where the ball landed and thought to myself that I'd probably never hit another ball like that again. And I never did. It was a once-in-a-lifetime swing. Later they told me it was one of the three longest home runs ever hit in Yankee Stadium . . . the 'House that Ruth Built.'"[2]

Charboneau continued to rake for power and raised his average to .354 by the end of April. He was becoming a full-blown folk hero in a town desperately yearning for one. His mark dipped to .265 on June 11 but rose steadily again as he maintained his consistency throughout the season. He slugged three home runs and drove in 13 during one three-game stretch that included a six-RBI performance in Seattle. His blasts came in bunches—Charboneau twice hit four home runs in seven games.

Thornton understood the impact Charboneau had on the community and the franchise, which had been searching for another Great White Hope since Rocky Colavito starred in the late 1950s. Colavito boasted the power and personality that had been missing ever since. Tony Horton had the power, but certainly not the personality fans could embrace. Thornton was not only introspective, but he was black. Others had come and gone and never captured the imagination of the fans nor hit with the authority of Charboneau.

"What you wanted was another Rocky Colavito," Thornton said. "That was what the front office and the fans dreamed he would become. Rocky was a good person, had charisma, hit a ton of homers, and had a great arm. Really, Rocky had far more ability and far more maturity than Charboneau. But Joe could have become an icon in Cleveland anyway. This is a blue-collar, shot-and-a-beer town. . . . The fans tried to make Buddy Bell into that guy, but Buddy didn't have the outgoing personality. They wanted Rick Manning to be him, but Rick just didn't have the ability. So they turned to Joe."[3]

And Joe responded by exhibiting his talent and flakiness. Fans were regaled with stories of Charboneau's past, such as the time he nearly gagged to death trying to swallow a whole egg in one gulp—shell and all. And the time he repaired a broken nose with a pair of pliers. And the time he wore a 99-cent tie with a shark on it to the 1980 Meet the Tribe banquet.

Charboneau grabbed a national spotlight. His on-field heroics and off-field adventures—embellished or not—were featured in the media coast to coast. He embraced the attention, giving those who asked for his time all they needed. He signed autographs for an hour before and after games. But Charboneau was far from savvy. He hired heating and cooling specialist Dan Donnelly, who had never represented an athlete, as his agent. Donnelly attempted to give his client a more serious image, but everyone wanted to know about the crazy side of Joe Charboneau. "I used to tell Joe that it was time to wipe the slate clean, to not dwell on those crazy stunts," Donnelly said. "I kept telling him that he was living what every kid dreamed, and he had to be careful not to screw it up."[4]

He screwed it up. Not intentionally, of course, but after finishing the 1980 season with a slash line of .289/.359/.488 with 23 home runs and 87 RBI to win American League Rookie of the Year, his career collapsed. Some have claimed he did not work hard enough to maintain his conditioning, eating and drinking too much. Charboneau insists that a back problem that began with a slide into second base during spring training of 1981 and exacerbated by trying to play through it ruined his career.

The downfall began in the offseason. The Indians hierarchy asked Charboneau to play winter ball in Puerto Rico in the fear that he would spend that time getting out of shape, but he refused. Charboneau, who spent the winter chowing down at sports banquets in which he was honored, eventually gained 20 pounds. But he has maintained that he arrived in spring training in good shape and that one fateful baserunning play planted the seeds of career destruction. "We were playing an exhibition game and I slid headfirst into second base," he recalled. "I felt something pop in my back. Originally, the Indians thought I just strained something. I hoped that was the case when I left the park that day, but by the time I went to bed, my back was so bad I couldn't move."[5]

Charboneau yearned to live up to the $75,000 contract he had signed during the offseason. He didn't want to use his back as an excuse. The back injury prevented him from using his legs and swinging freely. The baseball had no jump off his bat upon contact as it had in 1980. The result was a .210 batting average in the first half of the 1981 season, which was played in two halves due to a player strike. Charboneau failed to treat his back during the work stoppage and was demoted to the minors in August. He never recovered. Having lost half his salary to the strike, Charboneau fell about $15,000 in debt.

Back surgery brought a bit of optimism heading into 1982, but Charboneau seemed to embrace his image as a flake as much as he desired to rebound. He hit .330 in spring training but received little playing time once the regular season began. He eventually streaked his hair red to maintain his punk rock persona and descended all the way down to Double-A Chattanooga, where he went hitless in 13 at-bats and shaved his head. Despite signing with Pittsburgh in 1984 and participating in its spring training a year later, he never made it back to the major leagues.

In the end, all Charboneau had was memories. But time gave him a healthy perspective. He opened a batting school that he eventually sold and landed a job as a batting instructor under head coach and former Indians teammate Len Barker at Notre Dame College. It was Barker who provided Charboneau with what he claims to be his fondest remembrance as a major leaguer. It wasn't the three-deck blast at Yankee Stadium or anything about the Rookie of the Year season. It was playing the outfield throughout Barker's perfect game against Toronto on May 15, 1981.

"So, come the seventh inning, manager Dave Garcia went to Barker and goes, 'I'm gonna pull Charboneau in left,'" he recalled. "Barker goes, 'If you pull him, you'll have to pull me too.' I stayed in left field the whole game because [Barker] wanted me on the field. He thought everybody who started should be on the field if he pitched a perfect game."[6]

Charboneau told author Terry Pluto in the early 1990s that he remembered little about the 1980 season. He could not capture the experience for posterity in his own mind. "I felt like I was in a dream in 1980," he said. "But it happened so fast. I didn't enjoy it as much as people would think. I was worrying about staying in the majors, taking care of my family, trying not to mess up. I like it better now when I think back on it rather than when it was actually happening to me."[7]

The same could not be said for Indians fans. Though the memories of those who lived through it remain strong and the enjoyment Charboneau provided them in 1980 will always be appreciated, it could never top the joy they received when it was happening. That was when he was the beloved Super Joe.

CHAPTER SEVENTEEN

The SI Jinx or Crummy Pitching?

CALL IT A SURPRISE SANDWICH OR THE TEMPORARY AWAKENING OF THE Sleeping Giant. But 1985 to 1987 provided a roller coaster ride for the Cleveland franchise and its fans. It began and ended in misery, but it was like a fun day at Cedar Point in the middle.

The Indians "achieved" a rarity in those years with an above-.500 finish between two seasons in which they lost more than 100. They managed to pull it off with one of the worst pitching staffs in team history. But the bunch of that era will be remembered most for falling victim to the so-called *Sports Illustrated* jinx, a malady that has befallen dozens of athletes and teams featured on the cover of the famed publication. Indians outfielders Joe Carter and Cory Snyder graced the front of the 1987 baseball preview issue aside the headline "Indian Uprising" that promoted an article predicting the Tribe would win the American League pennant. What the crystal ball gazers at SI failed to consider strongly enough was their woeful hurlers.

A roller coaster begins with an ascension. The Tribe of that period did the opposite, dropping to the depths in 1985 before rising and falling again. The Cleveland team that launched that wacky period represented a new era under Peter Bavasi, who had replaced Gabe Paul as team president and chief operating officer in late November 1984. Bavasi was no greenhorn—he had already served as president of the Blue Jays and general manager of the Padres. He inherited the same problems that Paul could never overcome: lack of talent, lack of support, lack of money. But he also understood that Cleveland fans would flock to Municipal

Stadium at the slightest hint of a turnaround. And they would prove it in 1986.[1]

Paul and Phil Seghi did not dump only headaches on Bavasi. They had also engineered a series of deals for young position-player talent that created optimism. Among the shrewd and successful trades was the theft of center fielder and leadoff hitter Brett Butler and slugging third baseman Brook Jacoby for washed-up pitcher Len Barker; high-average, clutch-hitting first baseman Pat Tabler for nondescript shortstop Jerry Dybzinski; overrated outfielder Von Hayes for five players, including Julio Franco, who sprayed line drives all over the field; and strikeout machine Gorman Thomas for second baseman and offensive standout Tony Bernazard. They also pulled off a franchise-changing blockbuster, sending solid starter Rick Sutcliffe and catcher Ron Hassey to the Cubs for premier prospect Joe Carter and Mel Hall, who murdered right-handed pitching.

Indeed, the cupboard was hardly bare. And the starting staff would have boasted an ace had curveball specialist and future Hall of Famer Bert Blyleven not demanded a trade. The Indians yearned for Blyleven, coming off a 19–7 season in 1984 that placed him third in the American League Cy Young Award voting, to serve as a mentor in the youth movement, but he wanted nothing to do with the rebuild. Bavasi dispatched him to Minnesota in a dud of a deal that returned young pitchers Curt Wardle, Rich Yett, and Jim Weaver, as well as shortstop Jay Bell. Only Bell gained considerable success in the bigs—and that was after he was traded to Pittsburgh.

The influx of everyday talent could not transform the 1985 Indians into even a mediocre team. The 1927 Yankees could not have won with that pitching staff. They finished a bit below average in runs scored as Carter struggled and Hall lost the season to injury. With Blyleven gone around midseason and three starters owning earned run averages over 6.00, the Tribe were mashed into oblivion. Yet, under the radar, they played almost .500 ball over the last two months. Little could anyone have imagined, however, that the Indians were on the verge of their best season in nearly two decades.

Seeking desperately to revamp the pitching staff, the Indians tried to catch lightning in a bottle. They signed two knuckleballers in free agency—a young one in Tom Candiotti and veteran one in Phil Niekro. They traded for right-hander Ken Schrom, whose career had taken a wrong turn after one strong season with the Twins. And they hoped the young position players would take another step forward.

They succeeded beyond their wildest dreams in 1986. The Indians were transformed from doormat to mild contender. They led the American League in batting average, triples, stolen bases, and runs scored. Carter blossomed into a superstar by batting .302 with 29 home runs, 102 runs batted in, and 20 steals. Tabler, Bernazard, and Franco all hit over .300. The platoon of Hall and Carmen Castillo combined for 109 RBI. Jacoby batted .288 and finished second on the team with 80 RBI while Snyder showed promise. Candiotti finished 16–12 with a fine 3.57 ERA. Both Niekro and Schrom were at least dependable, and late bloomer Ernie Camacho managed 20 saves despite a terrible finish.

The Indians appeared dead in the water after a roller coaster May. A 10-game winning streak that ended on May 7 placed them in a flat-footed tie for the top but a 5–16 stretch in which they allowed seven runs per game pushed them nine games out of first place. The expected collapse, however, never materialized. The Indians won 26 of 39 to soar 10 games over .500 and pique the interest of fans, who began besieging Municipal Stadium. A packed house of 73,303 awaited them when they returned home from an 8–4 road trip on July 4 to face Kansas City. The fans got their money's worth when the Indians bolted to an 8–1 lead in the fourth inning and Niekro hurled a complete game for a 10–3 victory. A three-game sweep of the White Sox two weeks later pulled the Tribe within five games of the lead in the American League East. That "Indians Fever" song of the era in which every fan was urged to "be a believer in the Cleveland Indians"? Nobody believed it until 1986. Then everybody did.

"A lot of what happened that year did come from sheer emotion," Bavasi said years later. "The guys started to believe in themselves and what we were doing. They didn't think the Indians *had* to be a terrible team. We had players coming to the park at 2 p.m. for a night game and

Leadoff hitter Brett Butler bunted his way on base often during the magical 1986 season.

they stopped at the front office just to talk. We did things like putting air-conditioning in the wives' waiting room. That may not sound like much, but it meant a lot to the husbands because it made their wives happy. Several of our players had career years because we had a potent lineup. There was just a feeling of excitement."[2]

The Indians slipped along with their attendance in August and September, but the team drew almost 1.5 million fans that season, its top total since 1959. They had won 24 more games than they had the previous year. The emergence of top draft pick and flame-throwing southpaw Greg Swindell, who arrived to win five of seven decisions, added another reason for optimism heading into 1987.

But problems bubbled up beneath the surface. Not only was Swindell still far too inexperienced to count on and the pitching staff lacking in depth and talent, but after Jacobs brothers Dick and David purchased the team following the 1986 season, the Indians renewed Carter at just $250,000 when he requested nearly double that and eventually lowered his asking price to $387,000. Carter claimed that he remained unaffected by the contract squabble, but Snyder believed the team's refusal to pay a potential Most Valuable Player a bit more after a 121-RBI season spoke volumes.

"We've got such a good thing going," Snyder said, "why not pay a little more to keep the players happy? We're just talking about fairness, not millions. We can have a good team here for years. Why create a situation where as soon as a player gets the chance, he'll move out? That's not fair to the fans who've waited so long. I know I don't want to leave Cleveland. I love it."

Carter picked it up from there. "We've got a new breed of player now who actually wants to be in Cleveland," he said. "It may have started with [quarterback] Bernie Kosar of the Browns, for all I know. He wanted to play here. Other players are impressed with the way we've turned things around. We have a lot of players who were considered suspect as major leaguers on other teams—guys like Hall, Tabler, Brook Jacoby. We all took our bumps and bruises together, knowing we had nowhere to go but up. Now we're about to restore the history of the Cleveland Indians."[3]

Knuckleballer Tom Candiotti emerged as the ace of a weak starting staff in 1986.

No, they weren't. They succumbed instead to the legendary *Sports Illustrated* cover jinx. The famed magazine predicted that the Indians would win the 1987 American League pennant, but the players themselves knew that they simply did not boast the pitching to meet such lofty expectations.

The Indians made fools of the predictors and themselves from the start of that season, losing 10 of their first 11 to fall 10 games out of first in mid-April. They recovered to win 8 of their next 12, yet fell further back, then collapsed. They lost 12 of 14 just before midseason and crawled to the finish with a pathetic 61–101 mark. The Indians did not win three straight games until early July.

The offense that had led the league in scoring a year earlier placed third-last in that department despite fine seasons from Hall, Jacoby, Carter, Butler, and Tabler. But it was one of the worst pitching staffs in baseball history that doomed the Tribe from the start. Candiotti finished 7–18 and raised his ERA nearly a point and a half. Swindell won just three games. Niekro finally pitched like a 48-year-old. And the team yielded an AL-high 219 home runs. The Indians had descended from one of the most promising teams in baseball to the absolute worst.

And they weren't destined to get a whole lot better immediately. The failures of 1987 reverberated throughout the franchise for years to come. They strengthened the Jacobs brothers' plans to launch a youth movement. Even comparatively young players such as Carter, Hall, Tabler, Franco, Candiotti, and Butler were soon traded or allowed to leave in free agency.

But there was a method to their madness. The ballyhooed deal that sent Carter to San Diego netted catcher Sandy Alomar and second baseman Carlos Baerga, two players who would help the Indians finally rise to championship level. The front office made a commitment to unload players approaching arbitration and especially free agency while building their farm system and trading for young talent. The plan worked, as it produced such standouts as Charles Nagy, Albert Belle, Kenny Lofton, Jim Thome, and Manny Ramirez. Only then—and only after a new ballpark had attracted fans and badly needed revenue—did they spend on established stars such as Eddie Murray, Orel Hershiser, and Dennis Martinez.

Joe Carter slugged his way into the hearts of Indians fans in the 1980s.

Perhaps the collapse of 1987 greased the wheels for the wonderful events that followed. One wonders if the overhaul that transformed the Indians from perennial doormats to contenders would have occurred had the team taken another step forward that season rather than a huge step back.

CHAPTER EIGHTEEN

Heartbreak on Little Lake Nellie

THAT RARE, HEADY FEELING OF OPTIMISM HAD GROWN MORE PREVA-lent among Indians fans by 1993. Construction workers were busily building Jacobs Field after the albeit slim-margin passage of Issue 2 three years earlier. No longer did supporters in Northeast Ohio fear a relocation of the franchise.

Meanwhile, young position players such as second baseman Carlos Baerga and outfielders Kenny Lofton and Albert Belle had begun out-producing anyone who had worn a Cleveland uniform since the 1950s. Baerga was coming off a season in which he batted .312 with 20 home runs and 105 runs batted in. It had become obvious that the Indians had fleeced Houston in the deal that shipped catcher Ed Taubensee off for Lofton, who stole a league-high 66 bases and scored 96 runs in 1992. And starting pitcher Charles Nagy had earned a spot on the American League All-Star team.

Not that the pundits were about to pick the Tribe as a pennant contender heading into 1993. Certainly, *Sports Illustrated* wasn't about to venture out on *that* ledge again. The team had managed a record of 73–89 the previous season after sporting a mark of 57–105 in 1991, its worst since joining the American League 90 years earlier. As the city worked to shed its losing image through construction of the Gateway Project, which also would result in a new downtown home for the NBA Cavaliers, the Indians were toiling to rid themselves of the reputation as the Siberia of Major League Baseball. They believed that the new digs might attract better players to the North Coast—or at least keep those already wearing

Manager Mike Hargrove kept the Indians together after the Little Lake Nellie tragedy.

Cleveland uniforms around. They progressively and smartly launched a new tactic of signing their young players to more lucrative long-term contracts before their eligibility for arbitration kicked in.

Hopefulness permeated the team's 1993 training camp in Winter Haven, Florida. The Indians prepared to play their last season at crumbling Municipal Stadium and they yearned to make it a great one. Fans had grown a bit nostalgic over the old ballyard—the Tribe were about to play in front of their largest season attendance since 1949.

All was well—until March 22. That was the only off-day of spring training and the players sought to take advantage of it. Veteran relief pitcher Tim Crews invited several teammates for a family outing to his ranch on the shore of Little Lake Nellie in Clermont, nestled an hour north of Winter Haven. Some declined the invitation. Those who fatefully accepted were fellow pitchers Steve Olin and Bob Ojeda, as well as strength and conditioning coach Fernando Montes. They feasted on a barbecue dinner and watched their children ride horses from the Crews's stable. Then the players began discussing a boat ride on the lake.

Olin's wife, Patti, wasn't keen on the idea. It was getting dark, after all. And it was late—friends had been expecting her husband back in Winter Haven an hour earlier. He was supposed to meet best buddy and fellow reliever Kevin Wickander for dinner at 6 p.m. so the latter could present a birthday gift to Olin's daughter, Alexa. But nighttime bass fishing in Florida proved too inviting. So Crews, Olin, and Ojeda boarded the 18-foot high-speed craft with a powerful 150-horsepower engine. They had packed a cooler with a six-pack of beer and bottle of vodka. Olin embraced the opportunity—he loved fast boats and fast cars.[1]

Montes did not join them. His job was to fetch Perry Brigmond, a friend of Crews, and wait for the three to return with the boat and pick them up. It did indeed return—but with two physically dead passengers and another emotionally dead. Crews, whose blood-alcohol level was later determined to be over the legal limit in Florida, had steered the boat into the darkness and away from the porch lights that had provided greater vision. It slammed into a dock, decapitating Olin and nearly chopping the head off Crews. Ojeda, who later claimed that Crews was a "great boatsman" and that the throttle stuck, would have been killed as well, but he was apparently not holding his head as high. He was left to beg Crews in vain to stay alive and to wonder why fate had allowed him to survive and remember forever the gruesome details of such a terribly tragic event. He was not left unscathed physically, either. The dock ravaged the top of his head. Ojeda eventually lost consciousness, regaining it the next day, and asking his doctor, "Why didn't I get killed?"[2]

The calamity left one to wonder if it could have been averted had every set of circumstances not aligned. What if Dick Jacobs had not moved the team's spring training from Arizona? What if Olin, who had gotten lost on the way to the ranch, had returned to Winter Haven or at least heeded his wife's advice and remained ashore? What if manager Mike Hargrove had accepted an offer from the Dodgers to play an exhibition game that day? Far more chilling, what if more players and coaches had accepted Crews's invitation to his ranch and joined the others on the boat?

No speculation could bring Olin and Crews back to life and the Indians were devastated. They besieged the team psychiatrist, as well as roving psychologist Rick Wolff. "They had a chance to confront the situation and talk about their relationships with Steve, Tim and Bob," Wolff said. "It was real cathartic. The team's taking it hard. It's like two deaths in the family." Added a tearful Baerga, "What happened yesterday is kind of hard for our team. We lost two of our teammates. We have to keep going. The team is real down right now. The first thing we have to think about is their families."[3]

The gut punch indeed overwhelmed the Indians emotionally. They had hardly had a chance to get to know Crews, who had signed as a free agent just two months earlier. But Olin was a beloved figure, especially to Wickander, whom he had aided emotionally through alcohol rehabilitation. The side-arming Olin had emerged in 1991 as the team's closer despite a distinct lack of velocity and recorded 29 saves the following year. Olin retired batters on wile, a bit of late movement, and the courage to attack hitters with mediocre pitches. "He had the heart of a lion, the guts of a burglar," Indians general manager John Hart said. "He courageously threw that fringe stuff up there and got people out."[4]

Sidearming closer Steve Olin didn't have much stuff, but got by on guile until his untimely death.

Tim Crews was killed in the boating accident before he threw one pitch for the Indians in 2003.

The surviving Indians proved their closeness after the accident when 10 of them met in Charles Nagy's room for an all-night vigil. The entire team huddled around manager Mike Hargrove the following morning to cry and share their love for each other and those lost. Former Indians slugger Andre Thornton, who knew something about tragedy after losing his wife and child in a car accident, later gave an inspiring eulogy that brought tears to eyes and smiles to faces.

Hargrove spoke about the camaraderie of his Indians before their next exhibition game on March 25. "There's a tremendous sense of family here," he said. "It's a concept to take hold of. We have a lot of personalities and nationalities here, but what we have in common is a sense of responsibility to each other. We have problems like any team. But I can't imagine doing anything else, anyplace else, with any people other than these."[5]

The tragedy continued to test Hargrove, who was forced to keep minds on baseball when the feelings of loss and morose thoughts of grisly death permeated the clubhouse atmosphere. His task was impossible, and the Indians showed it on the field, falling hopelessly out of contention at 21–35 by early June. As if their luck had not been bad enough, they also lost Nagy for the year to shoulder surgery. But Hargrove and his players refused to fold. They won 13 of 16 during one stretch heading into Independence Day and remained within five games of .500 in early September. Their position player talent was beginning to overcome a lack of pitching.

The plan was working. And that plan included trading for young talent and rebuilding what had been a devastated minor league system. "I studied the Indians organization going back to the late 1950s," said general manager Hank Peters, who pushed the franchise in a positive direction in the early 1990s. "You can look back over 30 years and see the deterioration of what was once a great farm system. When the owners wanted to save money, they looked at cutting back the scouting and farm system because that was something the public or media couldn't immediately see. The other thing was that every four or five years, the Indians were sold. None of the owners made a long-term commitment. They just wanted to put a Band-Aid on the bleeding at the big-league level."[6]

The Jacobs brothers didn't bring along any Band-Aids. The result was a rich farm system that produced so much talent that it eventually allowed sluggers such as Brian Giles and Richie Sexson to be traded to supplement the pitching staff. By then, the Indians had established themselves as a perennial World Series contender. Some expected that to happen in 1993, but what happened instead on Little Lake Nellie made the team's last season at Municipal Stadium one to remember for a heart-wrenching moment in time that nobody could forget.

CHAPTER NINETEEN

Batgate

ALBERT BELLE HAD PROVEN TO BE MEAN, VIOLENT, IRASCIBLE, SULLEN, and vengeful well before 1994. But he demonstrated that year he was a cheater as well.

The Indians had given him a pass on all of it because there was something else he had established: He was arguably the most feared slugger in the sport. He stared menacingly at opposing pitchers, who had reason to be scared beyond that glare. Belle had emerged by 1992 as the team's best power hitter since the 1950s edition of Rocky Colavito. During the following year he ascended to all-around batting greatness, raising his on-base percentage 50 points to .370 while smashing 38 home runs and leading the American League with 129 runs batted in. He even stole 23 bases. Simply put, he had become one of the best offensive players ever to don an Indians uniform.

So the "incidents" were accepted as Albert being Albert. Punishments were sometimes meted out, but the Indians would not have dreamed of unloading the first player to ever slam 50 home runs and 50 doubles in the same season, lead his team to the pennant, yet fail to win the Most Valuable Player award because he was rottener to the media than to anyone else.

There was the time he grabbed a foul ball and fired it squarely into the chest of a heckler to earn a six-game suspension. There was the time he screamed at NBC reporter Hannah Storm for hanging around the dugout after batting practice during the World Series. There was the time he got into his truck and chased down teenagers he claimed had egged his house on Halloween. "You better get somebody over here," he told Euclid police officers, "because if I find one of them, I'll kill them."[1]

He never killed any kids, but he was sure busy killing pitchers in 1994, at least figuratively. Belle was on pace to achieve the mean 50-doubles, 50-homers trick and might have won the American League MVP had the lockout not wiped out the season on August 10 with the Indians—finally, finally, finally contending—just one game out of first place. And though he had become notorious for his temper, he had never taken center stage in an event worthy of an episode of *Mission Impossible.* That is, until July 15 of that year.

It was on that night that White Sox manager Gene Lamont, who had been tipped off that Belle hollowed out the barrels of his bats and corked them, approached the umpire in the first inning and accused the slugger of doing just that. Ump Dave Phillips took the lumber and locked it in his dressing room for later examination. Panic gripped the Cleveland dugout. Belle's teammates knew he corked all his bats. They were involved in the team's first pennant race in 40 years and could not afford to lose their premier offensive player to suspension. They had to get that bat back and replace it with someone else's, so they chose a Paul Sorrento model. But who would replace it? And how?

The who was relief pitcher Ross Grimsley. And he figured out how. He understood that the clubhouse and the umpires' dressing room were on the same floor. Both had false ceilings with removable tiles. A reconnaissance mission confirmed where the two rooms were in relation to each other. Grimsley realized that he could crawl atop the cinder-block walls that framed the rooms about 100 feet from the clubhouse to the umpire area.

Grimsley embraced his task. He loved adventure as a kid and this would let him be a kid again. So he grabbed a yellow flashlight and the uncorked bat, climbed with a still-unnamed accomplice onto the desk in the manager's office, and balanced himself precariously on the foot-and-a-half-wide cinder-block wall. It was hot. It was dark. He had to maneuver himself through piping that hung from wires. One slip-up and the pipes would rupture, snafuing the entire mission. He moved slowly. He required about 40 minutes to reach the spot where he believed the umpires' room to be. Like a super spy, he placed the flashlight in his mouth and pulled himself along on his stomach as he approached his ultimate destination.

After wrongly estimating his location, he removed a tile to reveal a groundskeeper, whom he fortunately did not disturb, sitting on a couch. He proceeded quietly to lift another tile leading to the umpires' dressing room. "My heart was going 1,000 miles an hour," Grimsley said. "And in I went. I just rolled the dice. A crapshoot." And if an umpire happened to walk in right then? "I'm nailed. I'm busted," he said.[2]

He nearly was. Soon after climbing from the top of a refrigerator and counter down to the floor, switching bats, removing all footprints, and returning to the pathway back to the clubhouse, someone entered the umpires' room. Grimsley was forced to sit for two minutes so he could not be heard. He rejoined his teammates, who expressed surprise and excitement over his ability to complete the secret undertaking. But it was also for naught. The bat he replaced the Belle model with bore Sorrento's name, leaving no doubt about the trickery. The White Sox complained bitterly as talk surfaced of bringing in the FBI—as if those folks didn't have anything better to do. The Indians were forced to return Belle's original corked bat. The result was a 10-game suspension that somehow was reduced to seven after appeal.

The Grimsley mission failed in its ultimate purpose, but he became a bit of a folk hero. Even opposing players were impressed. Included was White Sox catcher Mike LaValliere, who approached Grimsley standing with a couple teammates the next day. "Hey, I heard you guys had a mission impossible last night," LaValliere said with a smile. "That's beautiful."[3]

Belle continued to slug his way into the hearts of Cleveland fans. His cockiness and relentless attack on American League pitching captured the essence of the team's offensive dominance in 1995, a season in which they buried the rest of the division by Independence Day and finished with a .694 winning percentage, the best in major league baseball since the Indians finished 111–43 in 1954. Belle led the league in home runs (50), runs batted in (126), doubles (52), slugging percentage (.690), and runs scored (121), yet finished second to Boston first baseman Mo

That menacing glare of slugger Albert Belle scared pitchers—and so did his corked bat.

Vaughn in the MVP balloting. One was left to assume that those in the media angered by Belle's mistreatment of themselves and their peers refused to vote for him.

Belle would prove his superiority against Vaughn head-to-head in the first round of the 1995 playoffs, during which the latter went hitless. Belle slammed a game-tying double in the sixth inning of Game 1 off Roger Clemens and knotted the score in the eleventh with a home run off premier reliever Rick Aguilera. Boston manager Kevin Kennedy pulled a Lamont after the blast, asking the umpires to check the bat. In one of the most storied moments in franchise history, Belle rolled up his sleeve in the dugout, then flexed and pointed to his bicep, indicating that it was his muscles, not his bat, that sent baseballs deep into the night. "After the game they immediately sawed it open and figured out there wasn't any cork," Belle recalled. "It just got us fired up after that. We went on to whup them two [more] times and sent them home. . . . I was mad because they accused me of cheating. I told them, 'Hey, it's not about the cork in the bat, it's about the weight training and the long grueling hours I spent in the weight room.'"[4]

Belle would soon leave the Indians for the same White Sox that had instigated Batgate, but not before he launched one of the most epic home runs in franchise history. The 1996 Indians, who had lost some of the magic from the previous season, were on the brink of elimination in the American League Division Series against Baltimore. With the Tribe down 2–0 in games and tied 4–4 in the bottom of the seventh in Game 3 at Jacobs Field, Belle rocketed a grand slam to center field off Orioles fire-balling right-hander Armando Benitez to all but ensure victory.

It would be his last hit in a Cleveland uniform. Belle bolted for free agency in the offseason. He signed what was then the richest deal in major league history at $55 million over five years. The Indians pulled their offer to him four days before he committed to Chicago. Belle claimed he could have extracted more money elsewhere, but that he yearned to join a potent White Sox lineup—never mind that the Indians had easily outscored them in 1996 and boasted still-rising sluggers such as Jim Thome and Manny Ramirez.

Cleveland fans felt a sense of abandonment and anger when Belle left, as they would when Cavaliers superstar LeBron James bolted 15 years later. Indians supporters amid a 455-game sellout streak packed Jacobs Field as usual on June 3 for a battle against Belle and the Sox. They booed him relentlessly and showered him with debris, including Monopoly money, twice delaying the game. In his typical combative style, he motioned to the fans to continue the assault. When Belle fouled off a pitch in the ninth, a fan threw it back at him and missed by about 30 feet. And in just as typical an ability to rise to the occasion, he homered and doubled twice to lead Chicago to a 9–5 win. When victory had been secured, Belle gave the fans an obscene gesture before leaving the field.

Players on both sides defended Belle. "Out of anything you can say about the guy, he's a great player," said Thome, who would raise the ire of Cleveland fans himself six years later by leaving for Philadelphia before returning to their good graces. "And I think he really loves the pressure. I

The Indians erected a statue of all-time leading home run hitter Jim Thome in 2014.
WIKIMEDIA COMMONS, COURTESY OF ERIC DROST

really do." Added angry White Sox shortstop and future manager Ozzie Guillen, "Look at how much good this guy brought to this town, and the people forget that because he wants to make his living. That's ignorant."[5]

All that remained for Cleveland fans in their relationship with Belle, who lost his shot at the Hall of Fame when a bad back shortened his career, was anger and fond memories. In the end, however, the latter won out. Far more than the so-called abandonment, they would remember that intimidating stare at opposing pitchers, the flexing of the muscles, the baseballs soaring over the wall at Jacobs Field, the clutch blasts. Though Belle will also forever be remembered for the temper-driven outbursts, the passage of years has a way of making us all recall positive moments in time. And Belle, perhaps more than any other player, was responsible for ending two generations of futility.

CHAPTER TWENTY

The Mad Dash

DEATH COMES SUDDENLY AND BRUTALLY IN MAJOR LEAGUE BASEBALL.
Teams that win 100-plus games are often sent packing in the first round
of the playoffs. And it's over. All that work from spring training forward,
all those victories in the regular season become virtually meaningless.
Only one team celebrates after the last ball is pitched.

That fear was real for the Indians and their fans following Game 1 of
the 1995 American League Division Series. They blew opportunity after
opportunity at the deafening Kingdome against quite ordinary rookie
right-hander Bob Wolcott in one of the most frustrating games in franchise history. They wasted three no-out walks in a scoreless first inning.
They stranded two baserunners in the second. Paul Sorrento wrecked a
rally in the third with a bases-loaded double play. The Indians finished
with 10 hits and five walks yet scored just twice in the defeat. Kenny
Lofton reached base five times, but never home plate.

Fate and Lady Luck seemed to be pulling for the underdog Mariners,
who had overcome the Yankees in a dramatic Game 5 of the American
League Division Series while Cleveland was busy blowing out Boston.
The Tribe could have succumbed to the maddening way they lost the
opener and, indeed, destiny appeared to be working against them when
they followed a victory in Seattle with an extra-inning loss in Game 3.

But the Indians that steamrolled through the American League en
route to its best record in 41 years finally arrived. They swept Seattle the
rest of the way despite some harrowing moments, particularly in the
eighth inning of Game 5 at the Kingdome when two errors put a 3–2

Manny Ramirez came from the Big Apple to become one of the premier hitters of his era.

lead in jeopardy. Playing the role of savior was left-handed reliever Paul Assenmacher, who struck out super-dangerous sluggers Ken Griffey Jr. and Jay Buhner to preserve the victory.

Seattle was far from cooked—especially with imposing southpaw Randy Johnson hovering on the mound in Game 6. The 6-foot-10 beanpole with the fastest fastball in the game, once clocked at 102 miles per hour, allowed only one unearned run through seven innings. But fearless Indians starter Dennis Martinez, who was signed as a free agent in 1994 in hopeful anticipation of just such occasions, did better than match him pitch for pitch. He was hurling a shutout.

Then came the moment frozen in time that Indians fans will remember fondly forever. Catcher and ninth hitter Tony Pena led off the eighth with a ringing double to right-center. Lofton followed with a bunt single, sending pinch-runner Ruben Amaro to third, then stole second. With Omar Vizquel at the plate, a passed ball skidded by catcher Dan Wilson to the backstop. Amaro scored easily, and Lofton never stopped running. Wilson slowed his efforts after Amaro crossed the plate. Johnson stood idly by before he realized too late that the speedy runner had rounded third and was headed for home. Lofton slid past him, scoring all the way from second to give the Indians a 3–0 lead. The unnerved ace soon surrendered a home run to Carlos Baerga that knocked him out. The game was not over, but it was over. The two-run passed ball had pretty much clinched the first World Series appearance for the Indians since 1954.

Though Martinez pitched seven shutout innings, it was Lofton's mad dash that would become legend. Among those who would never forget was Indians general manager John Hart. "When Kenny didn't hesitate around third, it became one of the moments frozen in time," he said. "Your mouth is just agape. I remember thinking, 'Oh my God,' Kenny was just fearless." Hargrove echoed those sentiments. "When Kenny came around third, I was just as stunned as everyone else," he recalled. "I felt the blood rush to my fingertips. It was one of the greatest plays I've ever seen. I think the play just took the fight out of them."[1]

That's what Lofton had in mind. He was especially pleased to stick it to Johnson, who for reasons that remain mysterious did not like Lofton. He would often fire his lethal fastball up and in on Lofton, who did not appreciate what seemed to be obvious intent. One of those "Big Unit" heaters barely missed Lofton's noggin in the first inning of Game 6. "I closed my eyes," Lofton said. "I knew it was intentional. If you throw at a man's head, you could hurt him. That's life-threatening."[2]

Lofton struck out in that at-bat and again in the third, but pitcher Orel Hershiser and others worked to keep his spirits up. The encouragement paid off when Lofton singled in the fifth to tally the only run of the game until the eighth. Though his teammates believed Martinez and the bullpen could blank the Mariners throughout, that was a risky proposition. The Indians needed to put them away—and Lofton did just that

Leadoff hitter Kenny Lofton turned walks and singles into doubles with his speed.
WIKIMEDIA COMMONS, COURTESY OF JERRY REUSS

in the eighth with his bat and his legs. His sprint from second to home clinched it. "I was just going to fake it, but [Wilson] was taking his time," Lofton said. "I saw the catcher moving gingerly, and I felt he didn't see that I was going to go. I faked once and then I went."[3]

When it was over, the players celebrated like no other Indians had since before any of them were born. They were drinking bubbly, smoking cigars, hugging their wives, and getting a kick out of Bob Feller, who partied with them in a champagne-soaked T-shirt. Lofton spoke about what the triumph meant to the fans back home. "I'm glad for the city of Cleveland to be able to experience this, because they haven't experienced this for a long time," he said. "The city of Cleveland has grown a lot, and it's improving, and we tried to do this for the city."[4]

Indeed, one of the reasons the city had grown a lot was the heroics of the 1995 Indians, who lured fans both rabid and casual downtown to spend money in bars and restaurants, root their team to victory, and honk their horns in celebration. And though they lost the World Series to Atlanta in six games and could not win a championship in the years that followed, the Tribe of that era produced unforgettable magic, none greater than the mad dash from second to home by Kenny Lofton.

CHAPTER TWENTY-ONE

That "Vacant Look" in Mesa's Eyes

HALL OF FAME PITCHER LEFTY GOMEZ FAMOUSLY REMARKED, "I'D rather be lucky than good." The Indians did not have to choose in the late 1990s. They were both lucky and good. They boasted one of the premier teams in baseball during that era. But they were also fortunate that the competition in the Central Division proved unthreatening. Though team personnel never predicted division titles before seasons began—that would have been horrendously bad form—their fans began making playoff plans in March with nary a care in the world.

The Indians assumed the top spot on May 12 in 1995. They snagged the lead for good on April 13 in 1996. They took over first in 1997 on June 5. Incredibly, it took them one game to do the same in 1998 and four games in 1999. Their "battles" to win the Central were akin to those pitting the Christians against the lions at the ancient Roman Colosseum. But they underperformed in the playoffs, losing in the first round three times during that stretch, as well as in 2001. The only year in which they overachieved in the postseason was in 1997. That was arguably the most magical run of all—perhaps more so than in 1995.

The Tribe had been weakened offensively in 1997 by the losses of impending free agent Kenny Lofton, who was traded to Atlanta for fellow center fielder Marquis Grissom, and Albert Belle, though the addition of slugger and brilliant defender Matt Williams at third base, which pushed Jim Thome to first, aided their cause. Williams led the team with 105 runs batted in, but the team averaged more than a half run less per game than they had in 1996. And their pitching staff ranked ninth in the

American League in earned run average, greatly due to a starting rotation in which all five pitchers owned ERAs between 4.28 (Charles Nagy) and 5.65 (Bartolo Colon). Even closer Jose Mesa, who had set a team record with 46 consecutive saves, ballooned his ERA to 7.45 in early June and yielded the closer role to Michael Jackson before regaining it in August.

The result was that the Indians never got hot during the regular season. They posted an 18–20 record through mid-May and had managed just one winning streak exceeding three games on July 10. They stood at 57–54 a month later but owned a 3½-game lead on the rest of a pathetic division. After consecutive losses to Toronto, they held a team meeting to set realistic goals. They realized that they didn't have to own the best record in the American League to fight for a World Series title.

"The gist of the meeting was that we didn't have to win 100 games," Williams recalled months later. "All we had to do was be in first place at the end of the season. In the playoffs, anything could happen. Any team can beat any other team on any given day."[1]

What the Indians embraced proved prophetic. They clinched a playoff spot with a 19–9 run before finishing the season playing mediocre baseball. Most believed the Indians would be swept aside by the Yankees in the American League Division Series. But catcher Sandy Alomar had other ideas. The man who seemed to spend as much time on the disabled list as he did in the lineup had blossomed with opportunity, setting career highs in every statistical category and batting .324 with 21 home runs and 83 RBI to place 14th in the Most Valuable Player balloting. He had even slugged the game-winning home run in the 1997 All-Star Game at Jacobs Field to win the MVP of that contest. Alomar and the unlikely pitching duo of Jaret Wright and Chad Ogea were about to assume the role of playoff heroes for the Indians.

Alomar wasted no time flashing his heroics, blasting a three-run homer in the first inning of Game 1 at Yankee Stadium. But when ace Orel Hershiser fell apart and the Tribe lost, the pundits who forecasted an easy New York victory—perhaps even a sweep—appeared justified in their predictions. The teams split the next two games and the Yankees placed themselves on the doorstep of the American League Championship Series berth by taking a 2–1 lead in the bottom of the eighth in

Game 4 and sending greatest-closer-of-all-time Mariano Rivera to the Jacobs Field mound. But with two out, Alomar launched a game-tying home run into the right-field seats. And in the bottom of the ninth, singles by Grissom and Vizquel, the second of which took a fortunate bounce off pitcher Ramiro Mendoza and into the outfield, tied the series at 2–2.

Somehow, it did not seem too surprising that Alomar slammed the biggest hit of the year for the Indians. It was, after all, *his* season. "When [Rivera] came into the game, you thought the game was over, but that

Finally healthy catcher Sandy Alomar helped the Indians win the pennant in 1997.
COURTESY OF THE NATIONAL BASEBALL HALL OF FAME LIBRARY

was Sandy's year," Ogea recalled two decades later. "He had a great year and it was fitting for him to hit that home run and beat Mariano Rivera. . . . We got to him, which not many people did. The group of guys we had were veteran guys, that kind of stuff didn't enter their mind, it was like, 'Hey, we'll beat anybody they put on the mound.'"[2]

The Indians grabbed their momentum and ran with it. They bolted to a 4–0 lead in Game 5 and hung on for dear life behind Wright and Mesa, who retired five straight hitters, including three on strikeouts, to harken back his glory days of 1995. The Indians had upset the vaunted Yankees as fans whooped it up and honked horns in the streets outside Jacobs Field.

Revenge and redemption were desired and achieved in the American League Championship Series against Baltimore. The Indians yearned to avenge the first-round defeat to the underdog Orioles in 1996. And general manager John Hart wanted to prove wise the trading of Lofton for Grissom. The second allowed the first to come to fruition. Grissom batted only .261 and fanned nine times in 23 at-bats, but his three-run homer in Game 2 off Baltimore closer Armando Benitez turned the series around after the Orioles had snagged the opener. The Indians won the next two to set up a showdown between Charles Nagy and Birds ace Mike Mussina.

Nagy and the bullpen worked their way in and out of trouble throughout, allowing 10 hits and five walks in maintaining a shutout into the 11th inning. Veteran second baseman Tony Fernandez stepped to the plate against Benitez with two out and nobody on. Fernandez wasn't even supposed to be in the lineup, but a thumb injury to Bip Roberts, ironically sustained when he was hit by a Fernandez line drive in batting practice, necessitated his inclusion. "Tony Fernandez has put aside his ego, his personal interests," Hargrove said. "He has not accepted it with ease because he's a very good ballplayer. He's never complained; he has not been a clubhouse lawyer."[3]

Benitez tried to fire a fastball past Fernandez on the first pitch, but it stayed up in the zone. Fernandez slammed it into the right-field bleachers for the first run of the game and soon the Indians and the city of Cleveland were celebrating a pennant. "I have never been in this situation," said Fernandez. "This is what you dream about as a kid. I don't believe in destiny, but I do believe the Lord wanted this to happen."[4]

If only the Lord had wanted the Indians to win it all. Not that the team didn't enter the fray against Florida with a level of confidence not displayed at any point in the regular season. "This is a year where we didn't think we were going to the World Series because you don't know what's going to happen," Mesa said before Game 1. "Now we know we're going to win the World Series. The way this team is playing, no one thought we were going to play like that. We did it, and we're going to do it."[5]

Mesa didn't do it. His failures cost the Indians their first championship since 1948. They ruined the stunning performances of Wright and Ogea, who was on the verge of winning the series MVP until Mesa's Game 7 meltdown. Ogea pitched 6⅔ innings of one-run ball in Game 2 to even the series. Wright raised his postseason record to 3–0 by taking Game 4. Ogea allowed one run in five innings to win Game 6.

All the marbles were up for grabs in Miami on October 26. While Wright mowed down the Marlins, Fernandez played the role of hero again with a two-run single in the third. The Indians led 2–1 heading into the ninth. The World Series crown was so close they could taste it. So could the millions of Indians fans back home, eyes glued to their television sets. Vizquel approached the mound to visit Mesa, who had just entered the game. And the shortstop did not like what he saw. He wrote about what he perceived as a disturbing sight in the following passage from a 2003 autobiography titled *Omar! My Life On and Off the Field*: "The eyes of the world were focused on every move we made. Unfortunately, Jose's eyes were vacant. Completely empty. Nobody home. You could almost see right through him. Not long after I looked into his vacant eyes, he blew the save and the Marlins tied the game."[6]

Indeed, Mesa allowed two line-drive singles and a smash sacrifice fly to weak-hitting Craig Counsell that knotted the score. Fernandez went from hero to goat in the 11th when he committed an error on what could have been a double play, allowing the winning run to reach third with one out. Nagy then surrendered the game-winning single to Edgar Renteria, crushing the spirits of his teammates and Indians fans everywhere.

Jose Mesa was a lights-out closer, but he couldn't put the Marlins away in 1997.

Players shed tears in the clubhouse as media members on deadline scurried about, trying to extract quotes expressing the team's devastation.

Among the most distraught was Vizquel. "What's so hard is that we were one pitch, one batter, however you want to put it, from winning," he said. "We were so close. It's just so hard to describe."[7]

It didn't seem fair that Marlins fans, who had not fully supported their team and continued well into the next century to stay away in droves, jumped on the bandwagon to rejoice in the championship of a franchise that had been in existence a mere five years. Or that diehard Indians fans more than 1,000 miles north were forced to lament the lost opportunity to celebrate what would have been the team's first title in 49 years. So much for that parade down Euclid Avenue.

Indians players were not the only ones shedding tears on that painful night.

CHAPTER TWENTY-TWO

Return from the Dead

THE 2001 SEATTLE MARINERS WERE NOT EXACTLY CHOPPED LIVER. They were more like filet mignon. They owned an 80–30 record during a 116-win season when they arrived at Jacobs Field for a nationally televised Sunday night game on August 5. They featured one of the premier bullpens in baseball. So when they steamrolled to a 12–0 lead in the third inning and led 14–2 heading into the bottom of the seventh, a $1,000 bet on them would have likely returned about a nickel.

Folks scoff at that old chestnut about how it's not over until the final out. They figured the fat lady had gone beyond spraying her throat and practicing the scales by that point. She had to be singing up a storm. But in reality, she was still in her dressing room and had not crooned a note. Because the Indians proved on that surreal evening that it truly is not over until it's over.

What was about to be over was the Tribe's run of dominance in the American League Central. In a couple months they would lose in the first round of the playoffs for the second time in three seasons and launch a rebuilding process that resulted in just one postseason appearance over the next 11 years. The writing was on the wall—their aging rotation featured three hurlers with plus-5.4 earned run averages and the competition was finally starting to catch up. But the Indians still boasted enough bash in their bats to bludgeon the opposition. And that is what they did to the stunned Mariners, who were attempting to win their third straight in front of yet another sellout crowd in Cleveland.

Among the punching-bag pitchers was right-hander Dave Burba, who had followed three fine seasons with the Indians with a dud, after which he began to fade into the baseball sunset. Burba owned a fat 6.65 earned run average after he departed, having surrendered seven earned runs on seven hits in just two innings. Indians manager Charlie Manuel hadn't hoisted the white flag yet, but he did after Mike Bacsik arrived for his first major league appearance and poured gasoline on the fire. Soon top Tribe sluggers Roberto Alomar, Juan Gonzalez, Ellis Burks, and Travis Fryman were all cooling their heels on the bench.

ESPN analyst Rick Sutcliffe expressed mock dismay on the air over the brief outing of Burba, who hit the showers after three singles to start the third inning. He had allowed six hits and a walk to the last nine batters he faced. "That's the frustrating part for me as a young broadcaster," said Sutcliffe, who knew something about pitching, having won an ERA title with the Indians in 1982 and Cy Young Award two years later. "I did all of this work on Dave Burba today . . . I've got all this great stuff, and he's . . . gone!"[1]

Viewers were forced to speculate as TV cameras caught droves of Indians fans heading toward the steps. Were they leaving in the third inning? Were they all going to flood the concession stands at the same time to stuff their faces in misery? Did they all realize simultaneously that they had to go to the bathroom? Whatever the motivation, suddenly it no longer looked like a sellout throng at Jacobs Field.

The Tribe supporters certainly weren't inspired by Bacsik to return to their seats. He allowed four hits and a hit batter upon his arrival. Then, after Jim Thome at least gave those who stayed the chance to return home and exclaim, "We saw fireworks!" by slugging a two-run homer in the fourth, Bacsik gave the runs right back by yielding three straight singles. He finally stopped the bleeding as Seattle manager Lou Piniella begin giving his stars the rest of the night off. Out came hitting machines Ichiro Suzuki, Edgar Martinez, and John Olerud. Little could the intense skipper have imagined that they would be needed to avert disaster. After all, the Indians were getting nowhere fast against tough right-hander Aaron Sele.

Piniella allowed his starter to max his pitch count. Sele fired 116 before his removal after Indians all-or-nothing slugger Russell Branyan clobbered a solo home run in the seventh and his teammates loaded the bases. The Mariners were not exactly squirming when benchwarmer Jolbert Cabrera singled in two off southpaw John Halama to close the gap to 14–5.

That's when Rod Serling must have risen from the grave and appeared at Jacobs Field because an episode of *The Twilight Zone* was about to begin. Thome opened the eighth with a home run. 14–6. After a hit-by-pitch, Marty Cordova slugged one over the fence. 14–8. Einar Diaz and Kenny Lofton (who later stated he wanted to stay in the game because he possibly had a girlfriend in attendance) singled, then Omar Vizquel doubled. 14–9. "Hey, wait a minute, we've got a chance!" Lofton thought to himself. The momentum was halted when Lofton was called out at the plate after a wild pitch and Cabrera fanned. The Tribe trailed by five and it appeared their efforts would fall squarely in the frustrating "too little, too late" category. And when Mariners stud lefty reliever Norm Charlton retired two of the first three batters he faced in the ninth, it was obvious that the fans who had remained were headed for the exits.

Not so fast. Some turned back when Cordova doubled and Wil Cordero walked to load the bases. Diaz then singled to left. 14–11. Lofton, representing the tying run, singled. Up to the plate stepped Vizquel, who was struggling through his worst offensive season in a decade. A walk-off grand slam, which had occurred 13 times in baseball history to that point, seemed quite unlikely. Vizquel, after all, had just one home run that year. But Manuel gave his shortstop a more realistic goal to shoot for. "I told Omar if he went up there and stayed patient, 'You can triple into the right-field corner.'" Vizquel was quite skeptical. "I didn't really buy it," he said after the game. "I said, 'Yeah, sure, Charlie.'"[2]

Meanwhile, Piniella was forced to do some real managing after figuring logically that he could sit back, relax, and soak in another victory against a tough team on the road. He summoned closer Kazuhiro Sasaki, who was in the process of leading the American League with 45 saves.

Vizquel tried to follow his skipper's instructions, fouling off pitch after pitch. He worked the count full, then smashed a liner down the first-base line and into the right-field corner—just where Manuel called for it. A dive by first baseman Ed Sprague, who had replaced peren-

Brilliant shortstop Omar Vizquel developed into a dangerous hitter as well by the late 1990s.

nial Gold Glover John Olerud, came up empty as the runners sprinted around the bases. Lofton wasn't as fast as he used to be, but he reached the plate easily and pumped his fist in celebration. 14–14. The comeback was complete. "They are delirious in downtown Cleveland!" roared ESPN play-by-play broadcaster Jon Miller. Sutcliffe criticized Sprague for not positioning himself closer to the line. After all, only a double could tie the game.[3]

Sasaki induced Cabrera to ground out to end the inning, but the die was cast. The comeback allowed Manuel to summon closer Bob Wickman for a scoreless 10th inning and talented, but notoriously prejudiced, John Rocker to strike out the side in the 11th. When Piniella brought in control-challenged Jose Paniagua to start the bottom of the inning, what seemed inevitable became reality. He surrendered one-out singles to Lofton and Vizquel. Cabrera, not accustomed to the role of potential hero, swung at the first pitch, shattered his bat, and sent a Texas Leaguer into left field. The ball was hit softly enough despite its lack of depth to allow Lofton to try to score. Infielder-turned-outfielder Mark McLemore fired a strike to the plate, but the speedster slid under the tag of catcher Dan Wilson. 15–14. It was over. One of the most improbable comeback victories in major league history was complete. Celebration songs "Rock and Roll All Nite" and "Cleveland Rocks" blared from the speakers as the fans smart enough to stick around smiled all the way to their cars. The Indians had become the first team in 76 years to overcome a 12-run deficit and win.

"I can't explain it," Lofton said. "It was unbelievable. I've never been in a game like that in my life. My voice is gone from hollering so much. It was fun. Wow."[4]

The incredible triumph proved to be arguably the last hurrah of a golden era of Indians baseball. Cabrera claimed after the game that it would prove to be a turning point in what had been a mediocre season, but the Indians fell to the Mariners the following night to fall out of first place. And though they rebounded to win the weak Central Division easily, they lost in the American League Division Series to the same Seattle team they had humiliated two months earlier. This time the Mariners achieved the comeback, returning from a 2–1 deficit to advance to the

The Indians celebrate their incredible comeback defeat of Seattle in 2001.
COURTESY OF WIKIMEDIA COMMONS

ALCS. After exploding for 17 runs in Game 3 to place themselves on the precipice of an upset, the Indians tallied just three the rest of the way.

The era of greatness had run its course. Larry Dolan, who had purchased the team in 1999, spearheaded a rebuild. Gone in 2002 were superstars Lofton, Alomar, and Gonzalez. Vizquel and Thome followed them out of Cleveland the following year. The 455-game sellout streak was cooked as well. But the Indians did not fall back into any three-decade morass, as they had after the Rocky Colavito trade in 1960. New standouts such as sluggers Travis Hafner and Grady Sizemore and stud left-hander C. C. Sabathia would lead the franchise into a new, albeit short-lived era of prosperity, with another powerful push toward a championship soon thereafter.

CHAPTER TWENTY-THREE

Midges Are Our Friends

IT WAS A CROSS BETWEEN A MODERN-DAY HORROR MOVIE AND A 1950S science fiction flick. It could have been named *Night of the Midges*. Or *Invasion of the Lake Creatures*. Or *The Pests That Destroyed New York*.

The Yankees expected to be bugged by the pesky Indians in Game 2 of the American League Division Series on October 5, 2007. But they didn't expect to be bugged by bugs. And they were left to wonder which pests proved more responsible for a galling defeat that helped propel the Tribe to the precipice of their first World Series appearance in 10 years.

That the team reached that level proved the success of the franchise rebuild following the glory years of the 1990s and early 2000s. The Indians had returned to mild contention in 2004, ascending to within one game of first place in mid-August before a nine-game losing streak doomed their chances. They appeared destined for a playoff spot a year later, but a mistimed slump in late September and early October wrecked their wild card bid. They took a step back in 2006, but their patience and diligence bore fruit the next season. Veteran sluggers such as catcher Victor Martinez and designated hitter Travis Hafner teamed with emerging All-Star center fielder Grady Sizemore, whom White Sox manager Ozzie Guillen deemed the finest all-around player in the Central Division, to generate a potent offense.

At age 24, Sizemore had risen above the others. Martinez and Hafner were one-dimensional—tremendous hitters who brought little else physically to the club. Sizemore hit for power, stole bases, won the first of two Gold Gloves that year, and was so handsome that he attracted a

**Center fielder Grady Sizemore could run, hit and field until injuries short-
ened his career.**

fan group to the stadium that called itself Grady's Ladies. His modest nature refused to allow himself to acknowledge his greatness. "There is a superstar player on our team, but if you walked into our clubhouse, you'd have no idea who it is," said Indians general manager Mark Shapiro. "To watch him play day in and day out is a rare treat. All of us, from the front office to the players to the bat boys, are fortunate to see him every day. He is without a doubt one of the greatest players of our generation."[1]

The rotation boasted a more surprising rising star—at least that season. Starter Fausto Carmona, who it was later revealed was older than his claimed age and really named Roberto Hernandez, emerged from obscurity to compete for the American League Cy Young Award along with established star C. C. Sabathia, who won the voting. Carmona rebounded from a miserable rookie season in 2006 during which he lost 10 of 11 decisions, walked four batters per nine innings, and finished with a bloated 5.42 earned run average. His pitches gained life in 2007, sinking sharply down and to the left as hapless hitters flailed away. He finished the year 19–8 with a 3.06 ERA.

Among those most impressed was Twins star center fielder Torii Hunter, who spoke glowingly about Carmona after the right-hander hurled his first career shutout in mid-May to complete a three-game Indians sweep. "It's not normal," Hunter said of Carmona's sinker. "He's not even human. It's so scary. I thought I was hung over. . . . The dude is filthy. . . . If you've never played the game, listen to me. I'm a hitter. Right-handers have no chance unless they get lucky and get a hit on a broken bat."[2]

The combination of Sabathia and Carmona, along with smoke-and-mirrors closer Joe Borowski and a balanced hitting attack, kept the Indians in the pennant race into mid-August, at which point they took over the lead with a victory over Tampa Bay. They even went old school, bringing back Kenny Lofton for the stretch run. A short Detroit slump was all they needed to take control of the division. A 21–5 stretch culminated by a three-game sweep of the Tigers pretty much clinched the Central title. The Indians finished the regular season on a 21–12 blitz that provided momentum heading into the ALDS against the hated Bronx Bombers. One comforting thought for the Indians was that the

The power delivery of C. C. Sabathia, who won 19 games during the 2007 run to the playoffs.

series was scheduled to start at Jacobs Field, where they owned a 51–29 record. One discomforting thought was that they had lost all six games to the Yankees that year.

The Tribe left no doubt about the meaninglessness of the latter in Game 1. Sabathia struggled a bit, walking six and allowing three runs in five innings, but the booming bats still made it a laugher. They blasted New York starter Chien-Ming Wang and the bullpen for 12 runs on 14 hits, including homers by Martinez, Hafner, underrated first baseman Ryan Garko, and emerging rookie shortstop Asdrubal Cabrera. The Indians buried the Yankees with a five-run fifth and continued to tack on runs in a 12–3 rout.

Game 2 proved far tauter—and surreal. Only a third-inning blast by future Indians outfielder Melky Cabrera prevented Carmona from pitching a shutout. Meanwhile, veteran southpaw Andy Pettitte was tossing a shutout before giving way to promising flame-thrower Joba Chamberlain, who polished off the Indians in the seventh to maintain a 1–0 Yankees lead.

Then it happened. Tiny flying insects called midges attacked in droves. They were attracted by the unseasonable heat and humidity. They bugged the bejeebers out of the Yankees. "They just came out of nowhere," exclaimed catcher Jorge Posada. So worried was Chamberlain about the invasion that he carried a can of bug repellant to the mound with him for the eighth inning. New York trainer Gene Monahan arrived on the scene to spray his neck. It didn't help. He struggled to see Posada's target as the midges swarmed on his thick neck. It was like the Alfred Hitchcock movie, only with bugs rather than birds.[3]

The incursion had media members scrambling to study midges. Entomologist Ron Harrison offered that the midge was related to the mosquito but flew around more as pests than biters. He added that they bred on the outskirts of lakes during warm fall weather and that air currents off Lake Erie pushed them toward land that night en masse.[4]

Yankees manager Joe Torre learned later that the repellent Monahan used on Chamberlain had the opposite of the intended effect. "Little did we know that the stuff Gene was spraying on Joba's face was like cha-

Flash-in-the-pan Fausto Carmona, later revealed to be Roberto Hernandez, was struggling on the mound by the time this photo was taken in 2008.

teaubriand for those bugs," said Torre, who had contemplated pulling his team off the field and later regretted not doing so.[5]

That was more than could be said for crew chief Bruce Froemming, who never considered halting the proceedings, referring to the insect bombardment as "a little irritation." He added that "we've had bugs before. I've seen bugs and mosquitos since I started umpiring. It might not be a perfect scenario. Within 45 minutes, basically they were gone."[6]

That gave the bugs enough time to turn Chamberlain into Steve Blass, the famed Pirates pitcher who suddenly couldn't throw strikes. Chamberlain walked Sizemore and wild pitched him to second before asking for another spritz of spray. Two outs later, another Chamberlain offering went awry, allowing Sizemore to score and tie the game. Soon Chamberlain was spitting out midges like they were sunflower seeds. Perhaps the midges were Indians fans, having been born and raised in Cleveland, but Carmona retired the Yankees in order in the ninth under what appeared to be the same circumstances.

The Indians seemed destined to win, which they did when Hafner lined a bases-loaded single with two outs in the 11th inning. He was swarmed by his teammates just as the insects swarmed Chamberlain. The Tribe also seemed destined to take the series, which they did in Game 4 behind veteran right-hander Paul Byrd, he of the old-school full windup, and a 13-hit attack.

Tribe fans reveled in the defeat of the despised, ultimate-big-spending Yankees, but another major market team stood in the way of their team's first World Series appearance since 1997. That was the Boston Red Sox of future Indians manager Terry Francona. What appeared obvious was that the team required premier performances from the 1–2 punch of Sabathia and Carmona to overcome the big Boston bats. But appearances can be deceiving. The pair were both mashed in all four starts combined, yet the Tribe still should have won the series. Simply and most accurately put, they blew it.

The Sox slammed Sabathia for eight runs in the opener at storied Fenway Park. Uncharacteristically wild, the southpaw hit the showers in the fifth in a 10–3 rout. Carmona fared little better in Game 2, matching Sabathia with five walks and departing after four innings. But former

Red Sox outfielder Trot Nixon gave the Indians the lead in the 10th with an RBI single and light-hitting Franklin Gutierrez capped a seven-run explosion with a three-run homer to send the series back to Cleveland tied at 1–1.

The Indians took the momentum and sprinted with it. Heroes began to emerge, including unheralded starters Byrd and Jake Westbrook. Aided by a two-run homer by the rejuvenated Lofton, the latter blanked the Sox through six innings of a 4–2 victory in Game 3 before a raucous sellout crowd at Jacobs Field. Byrd did the same through five in a 7–3 triumph highlighted by Jhonny Peralta and Casey Blake blasts. The Indians were on the verge of an American League pennant with their co-aces rested and ready to go. They even had a chance to clinch a pennant in Cleveland for the first time since the playoff era began in 1969.

That's when they needed Sabathia and Carmona to shine. The former, who was badly outdueled by eventual ALCS Most Valuable Player Josh Beckett, yielded four runs on 10 hits in six innings of Game 5. Sabathia, however, made Carmona look like Sandy Koufax when the series shifted back to Fenway. The real Roberto Hernandez allowed four runs in the first inning and three of the six surrendered in the third as the Red Sox rolled, 12–2.

The hopes and dreams of the Indians and their fans boiled down to Game 7. Westbrook surrendered one run in each of the first three innings but settled down to blank the Sox over the next three while his teammates battled back. They cut the deficit to 3–2 heading into the seventh. Lofton landed on second on a one-out error, then Gutierrez whistled a hit down the third-base line. The ball bounced off the stands where they jut out. Lofton might have scored had he run backwards—he certainly would have crossed home plate with his speed, even at age 40. But too-cautious third-base coach Joel Skinner, who at first began waving Lofton home, then threw up the stop sign. Blake hit into a double play to end the threat.

Indians fans just added "stop sign" to the list of words that expressed their feelings of frustration over lost opportunities for their sports teams to win a championship for the first time since the Browns earned the NFL crown in 1964. Red Right 88. The Drive. The Fumble. The Shot.

Shortstop Johnny Peralta played a critical role in the Tribe success in 2007.
WIKIMEDIA COMMONS, COURTESY OF KEITH ALLISON 007.

The Mesa Meltdown. And now the Stop Sign. Skinner defended it after the game. "From ground level, with the ball shooting back behind the shortstop, no [I'm not going to send him]," he said. "In that situation, first and third, we're doing fine."[7]

Indians manager Eric Wedge showed his disappointment after the play to a national television audience as the announcers voiced their surprise. The ball had ricocheted far beyond the infield and Skinner had simply misread it. The inability to tie the game proved emotionally destructive to the team as they allowed eight runs over the next two innings in an 11–2 defeat. Game, set, match. Agony. The Indians and their fans were left with that gnawing feeling that a world championship had been there for the taking. After all, the National League champion Colorado Rockies had been cooling their heels for more than a week when the World Series began and were overmatched in a Boston sweep. That the Indians would have defeated Colorado as well seemed to be a given.

And when it was over, all they had left were memories. Manager Eric Wedge provided the media with a milquetoast speech following one of the most crushing defeats in franchise history. He spoke about what a great learning experience it was for his young team and how proud he was of his players. But reality told a different story. There is never a guarantee that any team returns to the playoffs—and the Indians did not play in a division series again for nine years.[8]

In modern parlance, it is what it is. A blown opportunity that Indians fans, with visions of that stop sign dancing in their heads, would rue for the rest of their lives.

CHAPTER TWENTY-FOUR

Backs Against the Wall

THE HISTORY AND DESTINY OF ANY TEAM ARE MARKED BY MAJOR MOVES both good and bad. Trades that go awry or are ticketed for greatness. Ownership changes that send a franchise reeling or soaring. Managerial moves that often also result in either consequence.

Indeed, a new skipper transformed the Tribe from an also-ran into an annual pennant contender in 2013 and beyond. Terry Francona, whose Red Sox had bounced the Indians out of the playoffs in 2007 and who had guided that team to its first two World Series triumphs in nearly a century, was attracted to the Cleveland organization. Upon losing his job in Boston, he corresponded frequently with Indians president Mark Shapiro and general manager Chris Antonetti. After the brain trust fired Manny Acta, only two candidates emerged as his replacement. They interviewed Francona and promising prospect Sandy Alomar, who managed the last five days of the 2012 regular season following the dispatching of Acta. It was no contest. When arguably the most successful and qualified candidate in franchise history wants a job, you give it to him. Francona was named manager on October 8.

"It's a good story, almost a family feeling," said Francona, who had worked one year as a baseball analyst for ESPN after losing his gig in Beantown. "I don't think you can take a job because of that, but it still means a lot to me. Because of Chris and Mark and my relationship, I am excited to try to . . . tackle every challenge that comes our way and do it together."[1]

Yeah, there were challenges. The Indians were coming off their fourth consecutive losing season at 68–94. They had finished second-last in the American League in attendance as fans had grown disenchanted and begun to feel the emotion that franchises fear the most: apathy. The hiring of Francona not only provided a manager with a winning pedigree but piqued the enthusiasm of the fan base.

Shapiro and Antonetti yearned to prove more. Criticized for skimping on payroll for a decade, the Indians spent money that offseason. They signed expensive free-agent hitters Nick Swisher and Michael Bourn to four-year contracts. And despite the disastrous results of those acquisitions—both performed far worse than expectations based on previous achievements—Francona turned ground round into filet mignon—or at least a nice T-bone.

The 2012 Indians spent nearly all of May in first place before falling apart and losing 15 of 16 to turn the season into a disaster. Francona and his front office compatriots had plenty of work to do, particularly with a pitching staff that had allowed the most runs in the American League. The emergence of Corey Kluber and a rare strong season from vexingly inconsistent Ubaldo Jimenez helped transform a terrible rotation into a strong one. Among those credited with the turnaround was pitching coach Mickey Callaway, who toiled with the complex, too-many-moving-parts windup and delivery of Jimenez and made him unhittable during the critical stretch drive in 2013. That Jimenez collapsed (again) after he left Cleveland for Baltimore in free agency proved the extent of Callaway's positive influence.

Though Swisher and Bourn vastly underperformed, they did lengthen the lineup. Meanwhile, Francona instituted a platoon system that helped the Indians average a half run more per game in 2013 and place fourth offensively in the American League. The respect the players gained for Francona inspired them to buy in as part-time players such as Mike Aviles and Ryan Raburn accepted their roles and crushed left-handed pitching.

Not that the Indians bolted out of the gate like Secretariat. Francona teams often start slow and the 2013 version was no exception, requiring a three-game winning streak to end April at 11–13. Hot streaks were

Nick Swisher smiled and laughed often, but didn't hit much during his stay in Cleveland.
WIKIMEDIA COMMONS, COURTESY OF ERIK DANIEL DROST

followed by cold ones until late September. An 18–4 blitz vaulted the Indians into first place, then an eight-game losing streak pushed them 5½ games out. They won 15 of 18 to return to the top and continued running hot and cold like a faucet through August, which they finished 8½ games out of first place.

What followed was a September to remember. With Kluber and Jimenez clicking on all cylinders, the Indians crept into the playoff race. They took 10 of 16 through the middle of the month as the competition jockeyed for position. The Indians also had to overcome shockingly poor attendance, impacted by a weak season ticket base negatively influenced by years of losing. A nine-game homestand in early September drew a mere 122,000—one game against Kansas City failed to attract 10,000.

But the Tribe worked to win over the fans. They needed every victory down the stretch. The most inspiring was achieved on September 24 against the visiting White Sox. The Indians trailed 4–3 heading into the ninth inning. With two out and one on, Francona called upon 42-year-old pinch-hitter Jason Giambi, who it seemed either struck out or hit a home run. Giambi, who had vast experience dealing with the pressure of pennant races and embraced his role as a mentor to the young players, smashed a no-doubter home run to right field to wrest victory from the jaws of defeat. The fifth consecutive victory moved the team closer to a wild card spot, but nary a slipup could be afforded the rest of the way.

"This is the stuff you dream about," Giambi told reporters after the game. "Coming down the stretch, trying to get a playoff berth. It doesn't get any bigger. It really doesn't. I'm speechless. . . . Right now, it's top of the world. I don't think I even touched the ground. They might have been able to appeal because I don't know if I touched any of the bases."[2]

The Indians continued to touch bases more than their opponents and touch base with their fans, more than 30,000 of whom came out to watch their team finish a sweep of the Sox the following night.

A four-game series at Minnesota to finish the regular season awaited the Tribe—and they needed all of them. The division title was out of reach, but they had forged a heated battle with Texas and Tampa Bay for the two wild card spots. Heroes emerged as the Indians were forced to overcome the sudden and inexplicable downfall of heretofore effective closer Chris Perez. Emerging catcher Yan Gomes slammed three hits, including a two-run homer, in the opener. Jason Kipnis singled, doubled, and tripled in an onslaught the next night. Back-of-the-rotation lefty Scott Kazmir pitched six brilliant innings, allowing one run and fanning 11, in a Saturday victory that placed his team on the precipice of a playoff spot. And Jimenez struck out 13 in a 5–1 triumph the following afternoon that not only clinched the wild card but ensured that the game would be played in Cleveland. In his last hurrah as a major league pitcher, Jimenez had gone 4–0 in September with 51 strikeouts in 41⅓ innings and a 1.09 ERA. Pure vindication.

"He went out there and pitched like an ace," Francona said. "That kind of typifies his season, you know last year he was the butt of jokes. But this year we end up arranging our rotation so he can pitch the game today."[3]

And as the champagne corks popped and the bubbly flowed in the Indians clubhouse, the always-effervescent Swisher stared at the television cameras and expressed joy and anticipation. "I'm telling you baby, we're bringing the wild card game back to the 216 [the Cleveland area code] and that place is going to be packed out and rocking, baby," he shouted.[4]

Swisher was right. The sellout crowd at what was now known as Progressive Field was indeed rocking and rolling in the Rock and Roll City. Francona surprisingly tabbed 23-year-old fireballer Danny Salazar to pitch against Tampa Bay. The rookie, who overpowered hitters in 10 starts, did the same early against the Rays. He ended the first inning by throwing a 100-mile-an-hour heater past James Loney and finished the first two with three strikeouts. But young Tampa starter Alex Cobb was equally effective, pitching in and out of jams. Meanwhile, his teammates began pecking away at Salazar. Delmon Young opened the third with a home run, then two singles and a double stretched the deficit to 3–0 in the fourth.

The Indians never recovered, blowing every opportunity. And it was the hitters wearing thin the patience of Cleveland fans that proved most infuriating. Shortstop Asdrubal Cabrera hit into a double play with the bases loaded in the fourth. Swisher grounded out with two on and one out in the fifth and fanned with two on and two out in the seventh, sealing the Indians' fate. Swisher and Bourn finished the game a combined 0-for-8.

The writing was on the wall for the two expensive free agents. As if the baseball gods were telling the Indians that they should not attempt to become big spenders, Swisher and Bourn were beset by injuries and poor production while continuing to spiral into oblivion. The former batted a meager .205 with the Indians over the next two years. The latter dropped in every statistical category in 2014. Most frustrating was that Bourn, who led the National League in stolen bases three straight years at his peak, even lost that ability with Cleveland. Both players were dumped in a trade to Atlanta in 2015 and soon out of baseball.

Shapiro and Antonetti could not be blamed for the signings. Their intentions were fine and neither player had given any indication of a downfall. Swisher and Bourn were the premier free agents on the market in 2013 and the brain trust yearned desperately to show a willingness to spend money. After all, the season ticket base was threatening to dip to about 4,000.

The acquisitions of that pair failed, but not the one that placed Francona into the manager's chair. And the Indians did not shy away from spending money within their budget as the team began to consistently thrive under the man they affectionately call Tito. Despite continued struggles with attendance, which albeit picked up in the coming years, the team rose to the middle of the major league pack in payroll by 2018. And though they lost the wild card battle in 2013, it was that season that launched a third era of greatness in Cleveland Indians baseball.

CHAPTER TWENTY-FIVE

The Merit of Merritt

A PLETHORA OF POTENTIAL PITCHERS PROVED THEMSELVES CANDI-dates to clinch a pennant for the 2016 Indians as the season progressed.

The most likely was ace Corey Kluber, who had won the Cy Young Award two years earlier and would earn another in 2017. But he won Game 4 in the American League Championship Series against Toronto and would be unavailable.

Another was fellow right-hander Carlos Carrasco, but a line drive that broke his hand in September knocked him out of the playoffs.

That it would be gritty Josh Tomlin seemed possible as well, but he had triumphed in Game 2 and manager Terry Francona preferred he not pitch on three days' rest.

The odds that left-hander Ryan Merritt would play hero were akin to those of the sun rising in the west. The rookie had pitched in four games with one start. His fastball could barely break an egg. He boasted pinpoint control, but seemingly retired batters with smoke and mirrors. But there he was, in Game 5 of the ALCS, on the road in Toronto, no less, making some of the premier sluggers in baseball look foolish.

The odyssey of the 2016 Indians really began late in a disappointing 2015 season, when they managed to dump the unproductive duo of Nick Swisher and Michael Bourn on Atlanta and chart a new course. They found a new power source in free agent first baseman Mike Napoli, who proved himself valuable on the field, pacing the club with 34 home runs and 101 runs batted in, and in the clubhouse as a team leader. Shortstop Francisco Lindor and third baseman Jose Ramirez emerged as two of

Indians manager Terry Francona is all smiles as he takes questions during the 2016 World Series.
WIKIMEDIA COMMONS, COURTESY OF ARTURO PARDAVILA III

the most exciting and productive young talents in the sport. And the deadline trade that procured unhittable southpaw reliever Andrew Miller from the Yankees—harkening fans back to a bygone era in which they sent standouts to the Big Apple for prospects—transformed the bullpen from fine to fabulous as closer Cody Allen and his drop-off-the-table curve were enjoying their finest season.

As proven typical of the Francona-managed Indians, they limped out of the gate, finishing April with a 10–11 record, falling six games out of first place in early May, and still hanging around .500 into June. But the cream rose to the top of a weak division. The Tribe embarked on what was then a franchise-record 14-game winning streak in mid-June, catapulting them into first place by seven games and piquing the interest of fans who had grown weary of their inconsistency. The production of one and all during the run reduced the pressure on everyone. "I know I don't have to be the guy," Lindor said. "Napoli knows he doesn't have to be the guy, [Jason] Kipnis knows he doesn't have to be the guy. No one here is saying, 'I have to be the man.' Everyone here is saying, 'Just do our job.'"[1]

The streak reached a crescendo, ironically as it would turn out, in Toronto, with a 19-inning marathon that resulted in a 2–1 victory. Carlos Santana, who was on his way to hitting a career-high 34 home runs, won it with a blast against Blue Jays middle infielder Darwin Barney, who was forced to the mound when his team ran out of pitchers. It seemed the Indians could do no wrong. Exemplifying the camaraderie and team spirit in that victory was starting pitcher Trevor Bauer, who offered to relieve to save the staff and threw five shutout innings for the win.

Cleveland finally lost the next night but coasted through the second half of the season with a comfortable lead in the American League Central. That would have afforded Francona the luxury of setting his rotation for the playoffs, but Lady Luck would have none of it. Third starter Danny Salazar was lost early in September to a strained right forearm. A smash off the bat of Detroit's Ian Kinsler broke Carrasco's hand two weeks before the playoffs. The old chestnut repeated by Boston Braves fans about the rotation beyond co-aces Johnny Sain and Warren Spahn in the 1940s came to mind: "Spahn, Sain and pray for rain." For the Indians after the losses of their second and third starters, it would have to be "Kluber and pray for rain, snow, and a 24-hour power outage." They were suddenly dependent on the annoyingly inconsistent Bauer and Tomlin, whose stuff was so unimpressive that he yielded homers in bunches and required precise control on every pitch to prevent a pounding.

A balanced hitting attack and the brilliance of Kluber, Miller, and Allen doomed the Red Sox in the first round. The trio hurled 14 shutout innings with 19 strikeouts against a Boston team that led the American League in runs scored. The Indians entered the ALCS with momentum.

Then the scientifically captivated Bauer haphazardly wreaked further havoc on an already decimated rotation. Bauer lacerated the pinkie on his right hand while tinkering with his drone, getting it caught in the propellers and requiring stitches. He was scheduled to follow Kluber to the mound but was pushed back to Game 3. After Kluber and Tomlin shut down Toronto in Cleveland to give the Indians a 2–0 series lead, Bauer arrived hoping that the stitches would prevent the wound from breaking loose. But after he retired two batters in the first inning, television cameras spotted blood dripping from his finger and onto his uniform. Bauer was forced to leave the game, but the best bullpen in baseball proved its depth by allowing just one of its own runs to score in a 4–2 victory that placed the Indians on the brink of their fifth World Series. "That wasn't the way we drew it up, but our bullpen—that's one of the most amazing jobs I've ever seen," said Francona. "If anybody has a hiccup, we probably lose."[2]

The soon-to-be American League Manager of the Year had a decision to make after the Blue Jays scratched across two runs against Kluber to survive the next night. He couldn't start Bauer. Tomlin was not rested. Carrasco and Salazar remained sidelined. Call it pulling a rabbit out of a hat, but Francona decided that painfully inexperienced southpaw Ryan Merritt would be that rabbit in Game 5. Merritt at least had some merit—he had allowed just two runs on six hits in 11 innings and beaten Kansas City in his only start. But the Royals were not the Blue Jays, and this was no meaningless regular-season game.

Toronto slugger Jose Bautista believed his team's lineup and pitching on the road with a Fall Classic berth on the line would overwhelm the rookie, whom he offered would be "shaking in his boots." But Indians teammates knew more about Merritt than did Bautista. "He's our secret weapon," said backup catcher Chris Gimenez. "If there's one guy that's not going to be rattled by the situation, it's him. To him, it's just another day." Added reliever Dan Otero, "Nothing fazes him."[3]

Perhaps it was because Merritt was not wearing boots, but rather cleats on the mound on October 19, but far more likely it was because he kept the free-swinging Jays off-balance with an assortment of slow, slower, and slowest fastballs, curves, and change-ups. Merritt retired the first 13 batters he faced (including Bautista twice), allowed two hits in the fifth, and left with a 3–0 lead. The bullpen did the rest, blanking Toronto the rest of the way. And when first baseman Carlos Santana drifted into foul territory to snag a foul popup off the bat of Troy Tulowitzki, the Indians were American League champions. Nobody received more credit or notoriety than Merritt, who became such a folk hero that Indians fans began buying gifts off his wedding registry. His contribution proved something about an Indians organization that only a few years earlier had been rightly criticized for poor talent evaluation and drafting.

"I think 'it' is the right word. We just have 'it,'" Miller said as the team celebrated the pennant. "Nobody's scared. We started a guy that had one career start today, and we had confidence in him, and I think that's special. It's just top to bottom, like I said, there's 25 guys, the staff, top down from ownership, the way they treat us is unbelievable. There's a good reason why we're here."[4]

A Cinderella series was about to begin. The Indians had not captured the ultimate crown in 68 years. But at least some people were alive the last time it happened. One would have had to be 108 years old to have been breathing when the Cubs won their previous title in 1908. Even as a team that had waited nearly seven decades to experience another world championship, the Indians could not gain the distinction of being the sentimental favorite internationally.

Not that it mattered on the field. The Tribe had won seven of eight in the playoffs and wasted no time administering a whupping to the Windy City boys in Game 1, scoring two runs in the first inning and coasting to a 6–0 victory behind Kluber as weak-hitting catcher Roberto Perez emerged as an unlikely hero with two home runs. Adding color to the broadcast were microphones on players. One was attached to Cubs catcher David Ross, who could be heard describing Kluber's slider as "filthy." The Indians ace had been baffling batters for years with the sharp, late movement on his out pitch, but the Cubs had yet to bear witness to it.[5]

Bauer, who donned the goat horns throughout the postseason and remained an enigma until harnessing his vast talents in the second half of 2017, was knocked out in a defeat the next day, leading to the tautest game of the series. Tomlin, who in an era in which even middle-of-the-road starters were heaving 95-mile-an-hour fastballs to the plate barely reached the upper 80s, got by on grit and guile again when the series shifted to Chicago. He blanked the Cubs with just one strikeout into the fifth inning, watched as a Coco Crisp single finally broke the scoreless

Tribe ace Corey Kluber uncorks a pitch in the first inning of Game 1 of the 2016 World Series.

WIKIMEDIA COMMONS, COURTESY OF ARTURO PARDAVILA III

tie, then gained great satisfaction over his contribution to a victory when Miller, Bryan Shaw, and Allen completed the shutout. The latter fanned dangerous Javier Baez with two out and two on in the ninth.

The Indians soon placed themselves on the doorstop of the World Series title and the city on the verge of a second celebration in four months after the Cavaliers had snagged the NBA crown in June. They dominated the Cubs in Game 4 behind Kluber as Kipnis blew it open with a three-run homer in the seventh. Francona was pushing all the right buttons. Faced with the choice of Santana or Napoli at first base in the National League park, he selected the former, whose three hits included a home run. He summoned Coco Crisp to pinch-hit for Kluber in the seventh and the veteran responded with a double that launched the three-run rally. And Francona continued to use the unhittable Miller to put out the most dangerous fires whenever they occurred rather than save him for the eighth or ninth inning. He was simply outmanaging highly respected and creative counterpart Joe Maddon.

The Cubs were healthier than the Indians and their depleted pitching staff. Folks had forgotten about Indians sweet-hitting outfielder Michael Brantley, who had missed nearly the entire season to injury. Yet Francona had his team on the brink of a world title. Maddon was famous for his ability to relate to his players and maximize their efforts. But the respect Francona earned had played a role in what was to that point a lopsided series. And the feeling was mutual. "I like these guys a lot," Francona said of his players. "They are very special. I don't think you have to have the stamp of a World Series on your team to feel this way. Sometimes things happen you can't overcome. They've done a really good job of overcoming a lot. But if it got to a point where it was too much, that wouldn't take away how I feel."[6]

Unfortunately for the Indians, it got to that point. Soon the loss of Carrasco and Salazar, which necessitated a three-man rotation, began taking its toll. So did the shortcomings of Bauer, who collapsed after three fine innings in Game 5, turning a 1–0 lead into a 3–1 deficit in a five-hit fourth that ended his night. The Cubs hung on for dear life as the desperate Maddon pitched closer Aroldis Chapman for 2⅔ innings to clinch a win that kept his team alive.

The series returned to Cleveland and Tomlin returned to earth. He fell apart with two out in the first inning, allowing four straight hits, including a solo home run to Kris Bryant. The powerful Cubs were finding their strokes against Tomlin, who surrendered bombs when he lost his pinpoint control (at one point in the 2018 season he had allowed 21 home runs in 42 innings). Francona removed Tomlin with the bases loaded in the third and Addison Russell unloaded them with a grand slam off Dan Otero. Game. Set. Match. A 9–3 defeat began draining the confidence of Cleveland fans. Now the series that could have inspired a joyous parade to honor their favorite baseball team, for which they had yearned all their lives, had come down to a coin flip.

One good thing. Kluber would start Game 7. One bad thing. He was only on three days' rest. The man lovingly nicknamed "Klubot" for his ability to focus and show no emotion on the mound had performed brilliantly throughout the postseason. Perhaps that would continue. Perhaps he was due for a dud. Nobody had a clue—but one came immediately when Dexter Fowler opened with a home run to center. It became evident that Kluber did not boast the sharp, late break on his slider that usually had hitters flailing away in vain. He was knocked out with no strikeouts after a Baez blast to start the fourth. And when even Miller allowed a run in the same inning to make it 5–1, the Tribe appeared doomed.

Not so fast. The packed house at Progressive Field that had been quieted didn't need scoreboard prompting to get loud. All it required was a rare two-run, bases-loaded wild pitch in the fifth and RBI double by Brandon Guyer in the eighth that cut the deficit to 6–4. Indians fans in attendance or watching on TV anywhere in the world would never forget what happened next. Up to the plate strode Rajai Davis, who as a power hitter would never be confused with Mantle—or even Napoli. With Chapman firing peas at 100 miles an hour, the possibility of Davis knocking one out of the park seemed to be slim and none—with none having gone home. But Davis sent a 2–2 pitch screaming down the left-field line, just high enough to reach the home run porch. Tie game. 6–6.

The place erupted. The decibel level was deafening. Suddenly, miraculously, the Indians were on the brink of a World Series championship. One more run, one scoreless inning courtesy of Allen, and about a million fans would be making parade plans. Twitter erupted. Major league players chimed in from everywhere. "Are you freaking kidding me?" wrote young Nationals star Trea Turner. "Omg omg omg I love baseball!!!" added Diamondbacks pitcher Archie Bradley.

Then it happened. Mother Nature reared her ugly head. A 17-minute rain delay after the ninth inning wrecked the Indians' momentum. Cubs outfielder Jason Heyward motivated his teammates with a speech in the clubhouse as the rain pelted down outside. Miller and Allen had already been used, forcing the less dependable Bryan Shaw to try to keep the Cubs' bats silent. No such luck. Ben Zobrist slammed a double down the left-field line and scored on a single to give his team an 8–6 lead. An RBI single by Davis in the bottom of the inning merely added to the frustration. When Michael Martinez—a defensive replacement and the Indians' weakest hitter—stepped to the plate, the ultimate defeat seemed a foregone conclusion. And it was. He dribbled the ball to third and was thrown out by plenty, setting off a Cubs celebration on the field as the Indians and their fans were left to lament losing what had been so painfully close. But the players spoke philosophically after the loss.

"Even when things looked so against us, it felt like there was magic in the air," Miller said, shaking his head. "Unfortunately, there wasn't quite enough."[7]

There never is for the Indians until they prove otherwise.

CHAPTER TWENTY-SIX

The Streak

IT HAS BEEN SAID THAT WHEN A PLAYER GETS HOT, HE CAN CARRY A team. That's one of those throw-away lines that please the ear but boast no validity. More than one major contributor is necessary for any club to go streaking.

Perhaps the greatest example in baseball history was the 2017 Indians. It seemed a different hero emerged every night as they established an American League record with 22 consecutive victories from late August to mid-September. Though the 1916 New York Giants officially own the major league mark with 26, their tie after No. 14 results in the Tribe owning the longest unbeaten stretch ever.

Their capability to pull off such a run appeared questionable through much of the season. The Indians struggled to pull away from Minnesota, which was finally providing competition in an otherwise horrible division. They ran hot and cold like a faucet through mid-June, at which point they stood at 31–31, two games behind the Twins. A four-game sweep in Minnesota put them ahead to stay, but a 48–45 record on July 19 placed them just a half game ahead. The Indians had bottomed out. The defeat that day came courtesy of frustratingly inconsistent short reliever Bryan Shaw, who turned a 4–2 lead into a walk-off loss that concluded a discouraging 1–5 road trip.

Most disturbing was a dormant batting attack that had scored three or fewer runs 11 times in 21 games with four shutouts. The hitters heaped pressure upon themselves, swinging consistently at pitches outside the strike zone and batting .209 with runners in scoring position during

197

that stretch. The lineup had been weakened by injuries to second baseman Jason Kipnis and right fielder Lonnie Chisenhall, who had been
leading the team in runs batted in. Manager Terry Francona, who rarely
expressed alarm, spoke about the need to break out offensively. "It makes
it harder to win," he said. "You're on the road to begin with and there's
just no wiggle room as we've found out. . . . On this trip it's been pretty
hard for us to score. We have to keep fighting. It's been kind of a theme
on this trip. It doesn't help to look back, but we just have to keep grind-
ing. Sometimes teams go through periods like this. We just have to figure
out a way to win 2–1 as opposed to losing 2–1."[1]

The Indians were simply too talented to be approaching the two-
thirds mark of the season barely over .500. Their Jekyll and Hyde offense
rose to life upon their return home from San Francisco. They averaged
7.4 runs in embarking on a nine-game winning streak, albeit against the
lesser lights of the sport. And when they followed with seven losses in
their next 10 games to drop to 62–54 with just 46 games remaining in
the regular season, an assumption that the Indians were little better than
mediocre would have been considered justified.

Then they got hot. Red hot. Scorching hot. The won eight of nine.
Then, on August 26, they embarked on a sizzling stretch the extent of
which had never been achieved in the American League. The Indians
emerged victorious night after night, day after day, They dominated.
They buried every hapless foe that stood in their way. They won by such
scores as 13–6. And 12–0. And 10–0. And 11–1. And 11–2. And 11–0.
They pitched seven shutouts, including three in a row for the first time
in franchise history since 1956. They scored nine runs or more eight
times. And when their 22-game winning streak finally ended with a 4–3
loss to Kansas City on September 15, marking their first defeat in three
weeks, they owned a 91–56 record and had all but clinched the division
championship.

It seemed a different hero emerged every game. There was little-used
Yandy Diaz smashing two doubles and a triple in a 13–6 bashing of Boston. There was forgotten Ryan Merritt pitching 6⅔ scoreless innings in a
blanking of Kansas City. There was designated hitter Edwin Encarnacion
singling and homering to help the Indians complete the first sweep of

three or more games at Yankee Stadium in 28 years. There were backups Giovanny Urshela and Abraham Almonte slamming key hits in back-to-back defeats of Detroit. There was hitting machine Jose Ramirez tying a major league record with five extra-base hits in a trouncing of the Tigers.

And there were the unforgettable moments that kept the streak alive. The run was in particular danger after 21 straight when they trailed 2–1 to visiting Kansas City with two out in the ninth and two strikes on Francisco Lindor, who responded by stroking a game-tying double to left. Newcomer Jay Bruce then won it dramatically in the 10th with a walk-off single down the right-field line. The Indians lost to the Royals the following night, but an appreciative home crowd responded to the end of the streak with a standing ovation that inspired the team to emerge from the dugout to acknowledge the love.

Francisco Lindor had emerged as a star by the time this photo was taken in 2015.
WIKIMEDIA COMMONS, COURTESY OF KEITH ALLISON

"They've been so supportive," praised Francona about the fans. "The atmosphere around here is incredible and I think our players wanted to show their appreciation. It's by no means the last game of the year or anything like that. It's just been pretty incredible how they've reacted, and we just wanted to show our appreciation because we don't take it for granted."[2]

Most impressive about the 22-game winning streak was the consistency of the pitching staff. Kluber allowed five runs in 39 innings with just two walks and 44 strikeouts to win all five of his starts. Carlos Carrasco surrendered six runs in 35⅔ innings, walked one, and fanned 39 in taking all four of his decisions. Emerging right-hander Mike Clevinger yielded just one run in 23⅔ innings with 28 strikeouts to post a 4-0 record during the blitz. Meanwhile, the one-two bullpen punch of Andrew Miller and closer Cody Allen proved unhittable. Though he was sidelined through most of the winning streak, the former pitched 8⅔ scoreless innings and fanned 17 from August 18 to the end of the regular season. And the latter was also unscored upon during the streak while racking up seven saves. It was no wonder the Indians compiled an absurd 1.58 team earned run average in those 22 games and held their opponents to a .251 on-base percentage.

As one might expect, the tear brought national attention. The Indians, however, downplayed its significance. "It's cool that we're winning a lot of games in a row, but we're not focusing on that," said Lindor. Offered Francona: "I think maybe this thing gets more carried away with other people, as opposed to us." Added Kluber after the team stretched the streak to 20: "We haven't talked about it at all."[3]

But *Sports Illustrated* writer Stephanie Apstein begged to differ. She claimed in a piece written in mid-September that the Indians embraced the record run: "Don't believe them for a second. Cleveland's win streak, which was laid to rest Friday at 22 games (in 24 days) old, mattered to the team. Why else would Francona run nearly all of his playoff lineup out there for a Wednesday afternoon game in September against the woeful Tigers, holding a 13-game division lead? Why else did they tear the jersey off rightfielder Jay Bruce—a Met 37 days ago—after he hit a walk-off double to beat the Royals, who haven't been a threat in weeks? They cared."[4]

Perhaps. But they certainly cared more about the looming American League Division Series against the Yankees. They performed down the stretch with the intention of heading into the playoffs with momentum. They won 11 of 14 to conclude the regular season with a 102–60 record and home field advantage throughout the American League playoffs.

It seemed Francona and the Indians could do no wrong. Even when he raised many an eyebrow by announcing that Trevor Bauer rather than Kluber would start the series opener at Progressive Field, it appeared to have all worked out in the wash. After all, Bauer proved brilliant, blanking the Bronx Bombers into the seventh inning before Miller and Allen shut the door in a 4–0 victory.

Game 2 motivated many to believe the Tribe were destined to win it all despite an ominous performance from Kluber, whose slider lacked its usual downward bite, leading to speculation that a sore back had altered his arm slot. The result was two home runs and a four-run third inning that ended his night with a 6–3 deficit. And when another blast stretched the Yankee lead to 8–3 in the fifth, the Tribe appeared doomed. That's when Lindor assumed the role of hero. His grand slam that smacked high off the right-field foul pole in the sixth made it 8–7 and ignited the sold-out crowd at Progressive Field. The Indians needed a pick-me-up after cleanup hitter Edwin Encarnacion had sustained a right ankle sprain. Francona placed the burden of emotional and physical leader upon Lindor. "One thing I said to him when Edwin went down," Francona related, "I said, 'Hey, we can't act like we got hit in the stomach and got the wind knocked out of us.' I said, 'Keep 'em going.'"[5]

Lindor did just that with one swing of the bat. And he appreciated the faith his manager showed in him. "It's an honor, it's a privilege, it's a blessing," Lindor said. "First, he has allowed me to be Francisco Lindor since Day 1. I'm usually the little kid that runs around all excited [that's] just in the big leagues playing the game of baseball. That's probably why he said that."[6]

The game of Home Run Derby continued when late-season pickup Jay Bruce cranked one in the eighth to tie it at 8–8. Each inning thereafter featured tense moments as the Yankees fought for their playoff lives. They put two runners aboard in the 10th, but Allen retired Chase Headley. The Indians did the same in the bottom of the inning, but defensive replacement Erik Gonzalez flied out. Two more Yankees reached base in the 11th, but Allen escaped again. Soft-tossing Josh Tomlin arrived to shut down New York. Then it happened. Indians outfielder Austin Jackson opened the 13th with a walk, stole second, and scored when light-hitting catcher Yan Gomes ripped a single past the bag at third. The Indians had stolen one from the Yankees and placed themselves on the brink of an American League Championship Series berth.

Surely, the Bronx Bombers couldn't recover from this one. They were a mess and manager Joe Girardi was being roasted in the Big Apple for a heinous mistake. He had failed to call for an official replay after Indians hitter Lonnie Chisenhall was awarded first base on a hit batsman just before the Lindor slam. Replays clearly showed that the ball never

Surprising Jose Ramirez displays the stroke that made him one of the top sluggers in the sport.
WIKIMEDIA COMMONS

touched Chisenhall. Under fire, Girardi admitted the next day that he had screwed up and accepted blame for the defeat. But that did little to soothe the fans, some of whom called for his ouster.

Most believed it was over. But they were wrong. The Indians collapsed as the Yankees fought back in support of their embattled manager. The Tribe committed seven errors over the last three games. They also stopped hitting, managing just five runs on 14 hits. Lindor and Ramirez banged out only two hits in 22 at-bats the rest of the way. And Kluber was knocked out in the fourth inning of Game 5, having allowed two more home runs in consecutive at-bats.

It had all been for naught. The streak. The 102 wins. The Game 2 comeback. The Indians were no upstarts after 2016. They were playing to win a World Series title. That added to the devastation of the ALDS flameout. "It absolutely stinks," said Allen, who surrendered two runs in Game 5 to allow the Yankees to coast to victory. "It's like being a kid going to an amusement park, and after 10 minutes you have to leave."[7]

Indeed, the series was amusing for the Indians and their fans for a while. But it ended in the same frustration that one and all had felt for nearly seven decades, since the last Tribe team celebrated the ultimate championship. It marked the second straight year that a three-game losing streak killed their quest for a crown. And all anyone could say were those familiar, hollow words: Wait 'til next year.

CHAPTER TWENTY-SEVEN

The Life and Death of Chief Wahoo

Baby Boomers remember like it was yesterday, waking up in the morning and seeing Chief Wahoo on the front page of the *Plain Dealer*. If they didn't already know, he would tell them if the Indians won the previous night. A smiling Chief with a lantern and raised finger signified a victory. A battered Wahoo with a black eye, teeth missing, and crumpled feathers indicated a defeat.

Nobody gave him a second thought. Heck, given the negative portrayals of Native Americans on television and in the movies during the 1950s and 1960s, that image of the wide-eyed, crazy-looking Chief Wahoo wasn't going to raise an eyebrow. Moreover, the logo was beloved by Cleveland fans. Those of all generations old enough to have seen the Indians play at Municipal Stadium recall fondly the huge caricature atop the ballpark greeting them as they approached. It is ingrained forever in their memories.

That love affair between Chief Wahoo and Indians fans clashed around the turn of the 21st century and beyond with the push toward political correctness. Even many who understood and sympathized with the centuries-long plight of the American Indian asserted that the Chief was nothing but a caricature whose presence did not in any way disparage that historically downtrodden group. Those who believed the team should rid itself of the logo used the eye test for their contention. "Look at the damn thing and tell me it's not demeaning," they would argue.

The Chief backers use the debatable claim that the nickname of the Cleveland baseball team was chosen to honor Louis Sockalexis, a former

Indians player of Penobscot heritage. True or not, that is unrelatable to Wahoo, who was designed by teenager Walter Goldbach after team owner Bill Veeck commissioned the logo in 1947, though a cartoon carried by the *Plain Dealer* in 1932 titled "The Little Indian" based on the result of the previous game featured a character that looked much like Chief Wahoo. The Goldbach logo, which he stated years later was not intended to offend anyone, gained popularity when the players wore it during their 1948 World Series victory. Though Indians pitcher Allie Reynolds was nicknamed Chief Wahoo in a *Plain Dealer* headline in 1950, the logo did not assume that moniker until 1952, when a person in a look-alike costume showed up at a party for dentists' kids at Public Hall.[1]

The image of Chief Wahoo remained virtually the same after his skin was reddened and his nose shrunk in 1951. And all remained silent for about a half century, though complaints from the moral wilderness could be heard occasionally. But times changed. Politically and socially aware Native Americans began showing up on Opening Day at Jacobs Field to protest the logo and the team nickname. The result was verbal clashes with fans, many of whom hurled insults or shouted obscenities at the protesters, having painted their faces red and adorning themselves in headdress or outfits depicting stereotypical Indians.

Many in the national media called for the organization to kill off the logo. Included was the Cleveland.com editorial board, which in 2014 wrote the following:

> *Many fans . . . view Wahoo through the lens of their youth, when they learned to embrace Wahoo the way they did Bugs Bunny, as lovable and funny, and before they knew anything about racial stereotypes.*
>
> *That's why benching Wahoo is so difficult for them. It implies that their affection for Wahoo was somehow impure. It taints their nostalgia. It creates a break from the past. For many, getting rid of Wahoo means giving into excessive political correctness.*
>
> *It's why this editorial board has hesitated in the past to take a position.*

But Americans have a long history of giving up on once-acceptable traditions when they come to realize the consequences—as unintended as they may be—of keeping them going.[2]

The pressure on the franchise eventually became overwhelming despite general fan support of Chief Wahoo. Major League Baseball commissioner Rob Manfred indicated strongly that he wanted the logo eliminated, especially if the Indians hoped to host the 2019 All-Star Game. The team announced early in 2018 that Chief Wahoo would be discontinued as a uniform or cap logo after the season, though it could still be sold at Progressive Field stores. That fans would continue to wear Chief Wahoo gear well into the next decade seemed a given. And that angered Philip Yenyo, executive director of the American Indian Movement of Ohio.

"They still want to keep hold of what they consider as their traditions and their history and they're not realizing that their history is basically a

The Indians killed off Chief Wahoo in 2019 to the chagrin of some fans and delight of others.
WIKIMEDIA COMMONS

history of oppression," Yenyo said. "I did say previously that it's a step in the right direction, but to continue selling the merchandise is like saying, 'OK, we realize it's wrong, but we're still going to make money on this.'"[3]

Though Cleveland fans railed against the official end of Chief Wahoo as the team mascot, national and international attention had grown increasingly negative over the years. But it was only a logo, after all, and some who claimed they would never attend another Indians game were certainly rooting from the stands in 2018. The only question that remained beyond the selling of Chief Wahoo gear at the stadium was what logo would replace him. It seemed most agreed that the "Block C" lacked personality.

That issue paled in comparison to how the Indians could beat the Yankees, Red Sox, or Astros in the playoffs and finally, finally, win another championship. One understood that no Cleveland fans would be railing for or against sending the Chief into the dustbin of history while they whooped it up at a parade celebrating a World Series crown.

Notes

Chapter 1: The Sinking, Stinking Spiders

1. Cleveland Spiders Team History & Encyclopedia, Baseball Reference, https://www.baseball-reference.com/teams/CLV/.
2. 1898 Cleveland Spiders Statistics, Baseball Reference, https://www.baseball-reference.com/teams/CLV/1898.shtml.
3. 1899 NL Attendance and Team Age, Baseball Reference, https://www.baseball-reference.com/leagues/NL/1899-misc.shtml.
4. Peter Cozzens, "Tangled in Their Own Web: The 1899 Cleveland Spiders, Baseball's Worst Team," Society for American Baseball Research, https://sabr.org/latest/cozzens-1899-cleveland-spiders-baseballs-worst-team.
5. Ibid.
6. David L. Fleitz, "The Corner of the Dugout," Baseball Almanac, http://www.baseball-almanac.com/corner/c042001c.shtml.
7. *The Sporting News*, https://sabr.org/latest/cozzens-1899-cleveland-spiders-baseballs-worst-team.
8. Bill Felber, "September 16, 1899: Misfit Cleveland Spiders Lose 24th in Row," Society for American Baseball Research, https://sabr.org/gamesproj/game/september-16-1899-misfit-cleveland-spiders-lose-24th-in-row.
9. Brad Herzog, "Hard to Believe How Bad They Were: The 1899 Cleveland Spiders Make the 1962 Mets Seem Like World-Beaters," *Sports Illustrated*, April 19, 1999, https://www.si.com/vault/1999/04/19/259642/hard-to-believe-how-bad-they-were-the-1899-cleveland-spiders-make-the-1962-mets-seem-like-world-beaters.
10. 1899 Cleveland Spiders Statistics, Baseball Reference, https://www.baseball-reference.com/teams/CLV/1899.shtml.
11. 1899 St. Louis Perfectos Statistics, Baseball Reference, https://www.baseball-reference.com/teams/STL/1899.shtml.

Chapter 2: The Loss of Joss

1. Paul Dickson, "The Tragic Death of Addie Joss and MLB's First Collection of All-Stars," The National Pastime Museum, February 5, 2017, https://www.thenationalpastimemuseum.com/article/tragic-death-addie-joss-and-mlb-s-first-collection-all-stars.
2. Alex Semchuck, "Addie Joss," Society for American Baseball Research, https://sabr.org/bioproj/person/5e51b2e7.
3. Ibid.

4. "Addie Joss" (obituary), *New York Times*, April 14, 1911, http://www.baseball-almanac.com/deaths/addie_joss_obituary.shtml.

5. Semchuck, "Addie Joss."

6. Ibid.

7. Addie Joss Statistics, Baseball Reference, https://www.baseball-reference.com/players/j/jossad01.shtml.

8. Wade Forrester, "October 2, 1908: Addie Joss Throws the Second Perfect Game in the Modern Era," On This Day in Sports, October 2, 2013, http://onthisdayinsports.blogspot.com/2013/10/october-2-1908-addie-joss-throws-second.html.

9. Semchuck, "Addie Joss."

10. Dickson, "Tragic Death of Addie Joss."

11. Ibid.

12. Ibid.

CHAPTER 3: TRAGEDY AND TRIUMPH

1. Gilbert King, "A Death at Home Plate," Smithsonian.com, May 9, 2012, https://www.smithsonianmag.com/history/a-death-at-home-plate-84826570/.

2. Ibid.

3. Tom Withers, "Chapman Plaque Key to Indians Success?" *Washington Post*, October 9, 2007, http://www.washingtonpost.com/wp-dyn/content/article/2007/10/09/AR2007100901579_pf.html.

4. Joe Sewell Statistics, Baseball Reference, https://www.baseball-reference.com/players/s/seweljo01.shtml.

5. Joseph Wancho, "Elmer Smith," Society for American Baseball Research, https://sabr.org/bioproj/person/d96af6d1.

6. "Unassisted Triple Plays," MLB.com, http://mlb.mlb.com/mlb/history/rare_feats/index.jsp?feature=unassisted_triple_plays.

7. Bill Nowlin, "Bill Wambsganss," Society for American Baseball Research, https://sabr.org/bioproj/person/420628e7.

8. Ibid.

CHAPTER 4: REVEALING RAPID ROBERT

1. "Population of Van Meter, IA," Population.us, http://population.us/ia/van-meter/.

2. C. Paul Rogers III, "Bob Feller," Society for American Baseball Research, https://sabr.org/bioproj/person/de74b9f8.

3. "Bob Feller: A Van Meter Legend," Website of the city of Van Meter, Iowa, http://vanmeteria.gov/visit/bob-feller/bob-feller-growing-up-in-van-meter/.

4. Frank Deford, "Rapid Robert Can Still Bring It," *Sports Illustrated*, August 8, 2005, https://www.si.com/vault/2005/08/08/8269207/rapid-robert-can-still-bring-it.

5. "Bob Feller: A Van Meter Legend."

6. Rogers III, "Bob Feller."

7. Deford, "Rapid Robert."

8. Rogers III, "Bob Feller."

9. Nick Acocella, "Rapid Robert Rocked 'Em with His Fastball," ESPN.com, http://www.espn.com/classic/biography/s/Feller_Bob.html.

10. Ibid.

11. Rick Swaine, "Jackie Robinson," Society for American Baseball Research, https://sabr.org/bioproj/person/bb9e2490.

12. "Bob Feller—Greatest Right-Handed Pitcher in Baseball History," Cleveland 101, http://cleveland101.com/cleveland-101-sports/bob-feller-greatest-right-handed-pitcher-baseball-history/.
13. "The Last Time the Indians Won the World Series," slide 10, CBS News, https://www.cbsnews.com/pictures/the-last-time-the-cleveland-indians-won-the-world-series-1948/10/.
14. "Bob Feller—Greatest Right-Handed Pitcher."

CHAPTER 5: THE CLEVELAND CRYBABIES

1. Bill Nowlin, "Ossie Vitt," Society for American Baseball Research, https://sabr.org/bioproj/person/128a662b.
2. Ibid.
3. James E. Odenkirk, *Of Tribes and Tribulations: The Early Decades of the Cleveland Indians* (Jefferson, NC: McFarland & Company, 2015), 124, https://books.google.com/books?id=ZEW7CQAAQBAJ&pg=PA124.
4. Ibid., 125.
5. Ibid.
6. Nowlin, "Ossie Vitt."
7. 1940 Cleveland Indians, Baseball Reference, https://www.baseball-reference.com/bullpen/1940_Cleveland_Indians.
8. Odenkirk, *Of Tribes and Tribulations*, 131.
9. Richard Scheinin, *Field of Screams: The Dark Underside of America's National Pastime* (New York: W. W. Norton, 1994), 212.
10. Ibid.
11. Nowlin, "Ossie Vitt."

CHAPTER 6: THE JACKIE ROBINSONS OF THE AMERICAN LEAGUE

1. Joseph Thomas Moore, *Larry Doby: The Struggle of the American League's First Black Player* (Mineola, NY: Dover, 2011), 39, https://books.google.com/books?id=UK7DAgAAQBAJ&pg=PA39.
2. Ibid., 40.
3. Ibid.
4. John McMurray, "Larry Doby," Society for American Baseball Research, https://sabr.org/bioproj/person/4e985e86.
5. Moore, *Larry Doby*, 42.
6. Richard Sandomir, "Cleveland Indians in 1948: A Story of Integration," *New York Times*, October 23, 2016, https://www.nytimes.com/2016/10/24/sports/baseball/cleveland-indians-in-1948-a-story-of-integration.html.
7. Craig Calcaterra, "When J.G. Taylor Spink Called the Indians Signing of Satchel Paige a Publicity Stunt," NBC Sports, September 13, 2013, https://mlb.nbcsports.com/2013/09/13/when-j-g-taylor-spink-called-the-indians-signing-of-satchel-paige-a-publicity-stunt/.
8. Sandomir, "Cleveland Indians in 1948."
9. Ibid.

CHAPTER 7: THE GREATEST TRIUMPH

1. Daniel Okrent, "Indians Summer: Lou Boudreau Had Indians Riding High in 1948," *Sports Illustrated*, May 31, 1999, https://www.si.com/vault/1999/05/31/261416/indians-summer-lou-boudreau-had-cleveland-riding-high-in-1948.
2. Ibid.
3. "The 1948 Playoff Game," Indians.com, http://cleveland.indians.mlb.com/cle/history/story2.jsp.

4. Ibid.

5. John McMurray, "Phil Masi," Society for American Baseball Research, https://sabr.org/bioproj/person/7981dd4f.

6. Bob Toth, "Veeck's Ownership Led to an Indians Championship Parade in '48," Did the Tribe Win Last Night?, June 22, 2016, http://didthetribewinlastnight.com/blog/2016/06/22/veecks-ownership-led-to-an-indians-championship-parade-in-48/.

7. "Veeck, William (Bill) L.," Encyclopedia of Cleveland History, Case Western Reserve University, https://case.edu/ech/articles/v/veeck-william-bill-l.

CHAPTER 8: THE MISTIMED SLUMP

1. Rich Exner, "Cleveland Weather History: Find Details for Any Weather Date Since 1871," Cleveland.com, September 5, 2008, https://www.cleveland.com/datacentral/index.ssf/2008/09/cleveland_weather_history_find.html.

2. "Experts: Recalling Mays' Catch," ESPN.com, September 29, 2004, http://www.espn.com/mlb/news/story?id=1891275.

3. Roger Kahn, "1 . . . 2 . . . 3 . . . 4 . . . & Bingo," *Sports Illustrated*, October 11, 1954, https://www.si.com/vault/issue/40768/17.

4. Jeff Merron, "The True 'Catch' Story," ESPN Page 2, September 29, 2004, http://www.espn.com/espn/page2/story?page=merron/040929.

5. Ibid.

CHAPTER 9: THE RISE AND FALL OF HERB SCORE

1. Steven Goldman, "You Could Look It Up: Herb Score," *Baseball Prospectus*, November 18, 2008, https://www.baseballprospectus.com/news/article/8318/you-could-look-it-up-herb-score/.

2. Harold Friend, "Herb Score Might Have Been the Greatest MLB Left-Hander of All Time," Bleacher Report, August 1, 2011, https://bleacherreport.com/articles/787667-mlb-herb-score-might-have-been-the-greatest-left-hander-of-all-time.

3. Ibid.

4. Daniel Wyatt, "Herb Score and 57 Years Ago," *High on History* (blog), April 26, 2014, http://danielwyatt.blogspot.com/2014/04/herb-score-and-57-years-ago.html.

5. Goldman, "You Could Look It Up."

6. As quoted by Goldman, "You Could Look It Up."

7. Wyatt, "Herb Score and 57 Years Ago."

8. Goldman, "You Could Look It Up."

9. Bill Lamb, "Gil McDougald," Society for American Baseball Research, https://sabr.org/bioproj/person/0c468c44.

10. Goldman, "You Could Look It Up."

11. Joseph Wancho, "Herb Score," Society for American Baseball Research, https://sabr.org/bioproj/person/1b133b89.

12. Ibid.

CHAPTER 10: LAUNCHING THE "COLAVITO CURSE"

1. United Press International, "Rocky Colavito Recalls the Harvey Kuenn Trade," *Los Angeles Times*, March 20, 1988, http://articles.latimes.com/1988-03-20/sports/sp-2150_1_rocky-colavito.

2. Terry Pluto, "50 Years Later, the Cleveland Indians' Trade of Rocky Colavito Still Stinks," *Cleveland Plain Dealer*, April 16, 2010, https://www.cleveland.com/pluto/blog/index.ssf/2010/04/50_years_later_colavito_trade.html.

3. Ken Coleman and Dan Valenti, *Talking on Air: A Broadcaster's Life in Sports* (New York: Skyhorse Publishing, 2000), 104–105, https://books.google.com/books?id=26UtAgAAQBAJ&pg=PT104.

4. Pluto, "50 Years Later."

5. Greg Popelka, "Tribe Game Vault: 4/19/60. Rocky Colavito Returns as a Detroit Tiger," *The Cleveland Fan*, http://tcf.danwismar.com/cleveland-indians/5-indians-archive/9266-tribe-game-vault-41960-colavito-returns-to-a-heros-reception.html.

6. Joseph Wancho, "Rocky Colavito," Society for American Baseball Research, https://sabr.org/bioproj/person/8899e413.

7. Ibid.

8. Ibid.

CHAPTER 11: THE SAD SAGA OF SUDDEN SAM

1. Pat Jordan, "Sam of 1,000 Ways," *Sports Illustrated*, August 17, 1970, https://www.si.com/vault/1970/08/17/611198/sam-of-1000-ways.

2. Ibid.

3. Ibid.

4. Russell Schneider, *Tales from the Tribe Dugout* (Champaign, IL: Sports Publishing, 2002), 125.

5. Joseph Wancho, "Sam McDowell," Society for American Baseball Research, https://sabr.org/bioproj/person/0c9cecef.

6. Terry Pluto, *The Curse of Rocky Colavito* (New York: Simon and Schuster, 1994), 91.

7. Jordan, "Sam of 1,000 Ways."

8. Wancho, "Sam McDowell."

9. Ibid.

CHAPTER 12: THE TRAGIC TALE OF TONY HORTON

1. "Steve Hamilton's Folly Floater," YouTube, posted by Frank Russo, July 19, 2010, https://www.youtube.com/watch?v=3RR2D5wdWIs.

2. Terry Pluto, *The Curse of Rocky Colavito* (New York: Simon and Schuster, 1994), 126.

3. Bill Madden, "Breakdown: The Strange Case of Tony Horton Remains a Mystery," *New York Daily News*, June 8, 1997, http://www.nydailynews.com/archives/sports/breakdown-strange-case-tony-horton-remains-mystery-article-1.755256#.

4. Pluto, *Curse of Rocky Colavito*, 127.

5. Madden, "Breakdown."

6. Scott Raab, "Taunting Tony Horton the Day after He Slit His Wrists: A Cleveland Fan Repents," Deadspin, May 26, 2010, https://deadspin.com/5548412/taunting-tony-horton-the-day-after-he-slit-his-wrists-a-cleveland-fan-repents.

7. Madden, "Breakdown."

8. Pluto, *Curse of Rocky Colavito*, 130.

9. Madden, "Breakdown."

10. Ibid.

CHAPTER 13: THE NIGHT THAT WILL LIVE IN INFAMY

1. Stefan Stevenson, "Watch the Rangers-Indians Brawl from 1974 Five Days Before the Infamous 10-Cent Beer Night Fiasco," *Fort Worth Star-Telegram*, May 21, 2018, https://www.star-telegram.com/sports/mlb/texas-rangers/article211615039.html.

2. Paul Jackson, "The Night Beer and Violence Bubbled over in Cleveland," ESPN Page 2, June 4, 2008, http://www.espn.com/espn/page2/story?page=beernight/080604.

3. Ibid.

4. Ibid.

5. Bill Lubinger, "Brawl Game," *Ohio Magazine*, June 2014, https://www.ohiomagazine.com/ohio -life/article/brawl-game.

6. Jackson, "The Night Beer and Violence Bubbled."

7. Anthony Castrovince, "Forty Years Ago, 10-Cent Beer Makes Memories," MLB.com, June 4, 2014, https://www.mlb.com/news/anthony-castrovince-forty-years-ago-10-cent-beer-makes -memories/c-78045480.

8. Lubinger, "Brawl Game."

Chapter 14: Putting the Cherry on Top

1. Greg Popelka, "Frank Robinson Arrives in 1974, Clashes with Gaylord Perry—Reliving Yesteryear," Waiting for Next Year, July 10, 2014, https://waitingfornextyear.com/2014/07/frank -robinson-arrives-in-1974-clashes-with-gaylord-perry-reliving-yesteryear/.

2. John Rosengren, "Crossing the White Line: As Baseball's First African-American Manager, Frank Robinson Furthered Jackie Robinson's Legacy but Failed to Fully Integrate the Game," *History Channel Magazine*, May/June 2007, http://www.johnrosengren.net/robinson.

3. Ibid.

4. Popelka, "Frank Robinson Arrives."

5. Rosengren, "Crossing the White Line."

6. Terry Pluto. *The Curse of Rocky Colavito*. New York, N.Y.: Simon and Schuster, 1994. 163.

7. Associated Press, "Controversy Still Swirls around Cleveland Indians." *Lake Charles American Press*, June 14, 1977, https://newspaperarchive.com/lake-charles-american-press-jun-14 -1977-p-27/.

8. Joe Jares, "An Indian Tomahawked," *Sports Illustrated*, July 4, 1977, https://www.si.com/vault/1977/07/04/621869/an-indian-tomahawked.

9. Ibid.

10. Ibid.

11. David Glasier, "Cleveland Indians: Frank Robinson Statue Unveiled at Progressive Field," *News-Herald*, May 27, 2017, http://www.news-herald.com/sports/20170527/cleveland -indians-frank-robinson-statue-unveiled-at-progressive-field.

Chapter 15: Drowning in Free Agent Waters

1. Mike Tully, "Wayne Garland Recalls His Historic Contract," *Los Angeles Times*, March 20, 1988, http://articles.latimes.com/1988-03-20/sports/sp-2144_1_wayne-garland.

2. Terry Pluto, *The Curse of Rocky Colavito* (New York: Simon and Schuster, 1994), 227.

3. Ibid., 228.

4. Ira Berkow, "Garland Eyes the Road Back," *New York Times*, May 10, 1982, https://www.nytimes.com/1982/05/10/sports/garland-eyes-the-road-back.html.

5. Tully, "Wayne Garland Recalls."

6. Ibid.

Chapter 16: Super Joe Charboneau

1. "Section 36: Go Joe Charboneau Song." YouTube, posted by booblikon, April 17, 2017, https://www.youtube.com/watch?v=S2JV0btxRvQ.

2. Paul Hofmann, "Joe Charboneau," Society for American Baseball Research, https://sabr.org/bioproj/person/f83534ac.
3. Terry Pluto, *The Curse of Rocky Colavito* (New York: Simon and Schuster, 1994), 209.
4. Ibid., 215.
5. Ibid., 217.
6. Michael Clair, "Meet Joe Charboneau: The Indians' Larger-Than-Life Cult Hero of the 1980s," MLB.com, February 2, 2017, https://www.mlb.com/cut4/the-legend-of-super-joe-charboneau/c-214075418.
7. Pluto, *Curse of Rocky Colavito*, 221.

CHAPTER 17: THE SI JINX OR CRUMMY PITCHING?
1. Roberto Dias, "The Cleveland Indians Thursday Named Peter Bavasi to Succeed . . ." UPI, November 29, 1984, https://www.upi.com/Archives/1984/11/29/The-Cleveland-Indians-Thursday-named-Peter-Bavasi-to-succeed/1043470552400/.
2. Terry Pluto, *The Curse of Rocky Colavito* (New York: Simon and Schuster, 1994), 266.
3. Ron Fimrite, "Pow! Wow! The Lost Tribe Is Back, Thanks to the Bats of Young Sluggers Joe Carter and Cory Snyder," *Sports Illustrated*, April 6, 1987, https://www.si.com/vault/1987/04/06/115165/pow-wow-the-lost-tribe-is-back-thanks-to-the-bats-of-young-sluggers-joe-carter-and-cory-snyder.

CHAPTER 18: HEARTBREAK ON LITTLE LAKE NELLIE
1. Bud Shaw, "A Moonless Evening, a Quiet Lake, a Tragedy: Recounting the 1993 Deaths of Indians Pitchers Steve Olin and Tim Crews," Cleveland.com, March 22, 2011, https://www.cleveland.com/ohio-sports-blog/index.ssf/2011/03/a_moonless_evening_a_quiet_lak.html.
2. Laura Lippman, "Relief at Last Intro: For Bobby Ojeda, Life Nearly Ended on a Florida Lake in 1993. It Began Again at Sheppard Pratt. Today He Plans a Reunion," *Baltimore Sun*, October 19, 1995, http://articles.baltimoresun.com/1995-10-19/features/1995292048_1_sheppard-pratt-bobby-ojeda-enoch-pratt-hospital.
3. Murray Chass, "Two Indian Pitchers Die, and Questions Emerge," *New York Times*, March 24, 1993, https://www.nytimes.com/1993/03/24/sports/baseball-two-indian-pitchers-die-and-questions-emerge.html.
4. Shaw, "A Moonless Evening."
5. Tim Kurkjian, "Tightening the Bond," *Sports Illustrated*, April 5, 1993, https://www.si.com/vault/1993/04/05/128320/tightening-the-bond-tragedy-drew-the-close-knit-indians-even-closer.
6. Terry Pluto, *The Curse of Rocky Colavito* (New York: Simon and Schuster, 1994), 285–86.

CHAPTER 19: BATGATE
1. Eric Schaal, "The Craziest Highlights of Albert Belle's Eventful Career," Cheat Sheet, March 26, 2018, https://www.cheatsheet.com/sports/mlb-the-5-wildest-moments-of-albert-belles-eventful-career.html/.
2. Buster Olney, "Yankee Ends Real Corker of a Mystery," *New York Times*, April 11, 1999, https://www.nytimes.com/1999/04/11/sports/yankee-ends-real-corker-of-a-mystery.html.
3. Ibid.
4. Paul Hoynes, "Cleveland Indians' Albert Belle: 'I Had Some Big Biceps and I Was Showing Them Off,'" Cleveland.com, October 3, 2015, https://www.cleveland.com/tribe/index.ssf/2015/10/cleveland_indians_albert_belle.html.

5. Associated Press, "Belle Shows Cleveland Why He's No. 1," *Los Angeles Times*, June 4, 1997, http://articles.latimes.com/1997-06-04/local/me-65347_1_dropout-rates.

CHAPTER 20: THE MAD DASH

1. Zack Meisel, "'Lofton Scores from Second,' an Oral History: 1995 ALCS Game 6–Cleveland Indians 4, Seattle Mariners 0 on October 17, 1995," Cleveland.com, October 17, 2015, https://www.cleveland.com/tribe/index.ssf/2015/10/lofton_scores_from_second_an_o.html.
2. George Vecsey, "95 Playoffs; Lofton Gets Angry, Then He Gets Even against Johnson," *New York Times*, October 18, 1995, https://www.nytimes.com/1995/10/18/sports/95-playoffs-lofton-gets-angry-then-he-gets-even-against-johnson.html.
3. Ibid.
4. Ibid.

CHAPTER 21: THAT "VACANT LOOK" IN MESA'S EYES

1. Jack Curry, "1997 World Series; Indians Went from Team in Disarray to Team of Destiny," *New York Times*, October 17, 1997, https://www.nytimes.com/1997/10/17/sports/1997-world-series-indians-went-from-team-in-disarray-to-team-of-destiny.html.
2. Anna McDonald, "Postseason Highlight and Heartache: 1997 Cleveland Indians," ESPN.com, October 7, 2016, http://www.espn.com/mlb/story/_/id/17730569/postseason-highlight-heartache-1997-cleveland-indians.
3. George Vecsey, "Sports of the Times; Fernandez Did Damage Both Ways," *New York Times*, October 17, 1997, https://www.nytimes.com/1997/10/16/sports/sports-of-the-times-fernandez-did-damage-both-ways.html.
4. Ibid.
5. Curry, "1997 World Series."
6. Omar Vizquel, *Omar! My Life On and Off the Field* (Cleveland, OH: Gray & Company, 2003), 13.
7. Tom Verducci, "Happy Ending," *Sports Illustrated*, November 3, 1997, https://www.si.com/vault/1997/11/03/234198/happy-ending-the-marlins-stirring-11th-inning-come-from-behind-defeat-of-the-indians-in-game-7-redeemed-an-otherwise-lackluster-series.

CHAPTER 22: RETURN FROM THE DEAD

1. Paul Blest, "The Improbable Story of Baseball's Wildest Comeback," *Deadspin*, August 5, 2015, https://deadspin.com/the-improbable-story-of-baseballs-wildest-comeback-1721720709.
2. Tom Withers, "The Majors: M's Blow Mother of All Leads," *Kitsap Sun*, August 6, 2001, https://products.kitsapsun.com/archive/2001/08-06/0014_the_majors__m_s_blow_mother_of_al.html.
3. Blest, "The Improbable Story."
4. Associated Press, "Indians Erase 12–0 Deficit in Victory," *Los Angeles Times*, August 6, 2001, http://articles.latimes.com/2001/aug/06/sports/sp-31176.

CHAPTER 23: MIDGES ARE OUR FRIENDS

1. Tom Verducci, "One Sizemore Fits All," *Sports Illustrated*, May 14, 2007, https://www.si.com/vault/2007/05/14/100030481/one-sizemore-fits-all.

2. Tom Withers, "Carmona Blanks Twins for His 1st Shutout," *Washington Post*, May 17, 2007, http://www.washingtonpost.com/wp-dyn/content/article/2007/05/17/AR2007051701365_pf.html.

3. Associated Press, "The Bugs Who Ate the Yankees," CBS News, October 6, 2007, https://www.cbsnews.com/news/the-bugs-who-ate-the-yankees/.

4. Ibid.

5. Ken Davidoff and George A. King III, "The Night When Bugs Changed the Course of Yankees History," *New York Post*, October 4, 2017, https://nypost.com/2017/10/04/the-night-when-bugs-changed-the-course-of-yankees-history/.

6. Associated Press, "The Bugs Who Ate the Yankees."

7. John Harper, "Indians Blow 3–1 Lead to Red Sox and Go from Bad to Cursed," *New York Daily News*, October 22, 2007, http://www.nydailynews.com/sports/baseball/indians-blow-3-1-lead-red-sox-bad-cursed-article-1.228367#.

8. Mike Shalin, "Red Sox Crush Indians to Reach World Series," Reuters, October 22, 2007, https://www.reuters.com/article/us-baseball-american-sunday-idUSB45944420071022.

Chapter 24: Backs Against the Wall

1. Associated Press, "Terry Francona to Take Over Indians," ESPN.com, October 6, 2012, http://www.espn.com/mlb/story/_/id/8470798/terry-francona-named-new-manager-cleveland-indians.

2. Paul Hoynes, "Jason Giambi Saves Cleveland Indians with Game-Winning Homer in 5–4 Win over White Sox," Cleveland.com, https://www.cleveland.com/tribe/index.ssf/2013/09/jason_giambi_saves_cleveland_i.html.

3. Paul Hoynes, "Ubaldo Jimenez Strikes Out 13 as Cleveland Indians Claim Wild-Card Spot with 5–1 Win over Twins," Cleveland.com, September 30, 2013, https://www.cleveland.com/tribe/index.ssf/2013/09/ubaldo_jimenez_strikes_out_13.html.

4. Ibid.

Chapter 25: The Merit of Merritt

1. Ray Glier, "Indians Beat Braves for Longest Winning Streak in 34 Years," *USA Today*, June 28, 2016, https://www.usatoday.com/story/sports/mlb/2016/06/28/kluber-indians-beat-braves-5-3-for-11th-straight-win/86497336/.

2. Paul Hoynes, "Cleveland Indians on Verge of the World Series with 4–2 Win over Toronto in Game 3 of ALCS," Cleveland.com, October 17, 2016, https://www.cleveland.com/tribe/index.ssf/2016/10/cleveland_indians_toronto_blue_47.html.

3. Mike Axisa, "Jays' Bautista Says Merritt Will Be 'Shaking in His Boots,' Indians Not Concerned," MLB.com, October 19, 2016, https://www.cbssports.com/mlb/news/jays-bautista-says-merritt-will-be-shaking-in-his-boots-indians-not-concerned/.

4. Jordan Bastian and Gregor Chisholm, "Tribe in World Series: Better Relieve It!" MLB.com, October 20, 2016, https://www.mlb.com/indians/news/indians-beat-blue-jays-to-win-al-pennant/c-206599252.

5. Ben Lindbergh, "Cleveland's Holy October Pitching Trinity Did It Again," The Ringer, October 26, 2016, https://www.theringer.com/2016/10/26/16042648/2016-world-series-game-1-cleveland-indians-chicago-cubs-corey-kluber-26bf4029524a.

6. Thomas Boswell, "Terry Francona Is Pushing All the Right Buttons in World Series," *Washington Post*, October 29, 2016, https://www.washingtonpost.com/sports/nationals/terry-francona-is-pushing-all-the-right-buttons-in-world-series/2016/10/29/6792f836-9d56-11e6-9980-50913d68eacb_story.html.

7. Stephanie Apstein, "Indians' Title Hopes Dashed as Their Magic Runs Out in Game 7 Loss," *Sports Illustrated*, November 3, 2016, https://www.si.com/mlb/2016/11/03/world-series-game-7-cubs-indians-corey-kluber-andrew-miller.

CHAPTER 26: THE STREAK

1. Paul Hoynes, "Cleveland Indians' Offense Sends Up a Flare as Trading Deadline Draws Near," Cleveland.com, July 19, 2017, https://www.cleveland.com/tribe/index.ssf/2017/07/post_524.html#incart_big-photo.
2. Tom Withers, "22 and Through: Indians' AL Record Win Streak Stopped at 22," NBC Sports Philadelphia, September 15, 2017, http://scores.nbcsportsphiladelphia.com/mlb/recap.asp?lg=MLB&g=370915105.
3. Stephanie Apstein, "Even If Indians Players Won't Admit It, the 22-Game Win Streak Meant Plenty to the Organization," *Sports Illustrated*, September 16, 2017, https://www.si.com/mlb/2017/09/16/cleveland-indians-22-game-win-streak-means-plenty.
4. Ibid.
5. William Kosileski, "Trusted Lindor Steps Up as Leader, Hits Slam," MLB.com, October 8, 2017, https://www.mlb.com/news/francisco-lindors-grand-slam-sparks-indians/c-257695068.
6. Ibid.
7. David Waldstein, "What Happened to the Cleveland Indians?" *New York Times*, October 12, 2017, https://www.nytimes.com/2017/10/12/sports/baseball/cleveland-indians-playoffs.html.

CHAPTER 27: THE LIFE AND DEATH OF CHIEF WAHOO

1. Brad Ricca, "The Secret History of Chief Wahoo," *Belt Magazine*, June 19, 2014, http://beltmag.com/secret-history-chief-wahoo/.
2. Editorial Board, "The Tribe Should Retire Chief Wahoo Once and For All," Cleveland.com, February 28, 2014, https://www.cleveland.com/opinion/index.ssf/2014/02/the_tribe_should_retire_chief.html.
3. Mark Townsend, "Tensions Run High as Chief Wahoo Debate Continues at Indians Home Opener," Yahoo! Sports, April 6, 2018, https://sports.yahoo.com/tensions-run-high-chief-wahoo-debate-continues-indians-home-opener-014939668.html.